Two
Careers—
One
Marriage

Two Careers—
One
Marriage

William M. Jones and Ruth A. Jones

amacom

A Division of American Management Associations

Library of Congress Cataloging in Publication Data

Jones, William McKendrey.
    Two careers—one marriage.

    Includes index.
    1. Married people—Employment—United States.
2. Choice (Psychology) 3. Interpersonal relations.
I. Jones, Ruth Ann, 1928-   joint author. II. Title.
HQ734.J63   301.42   79-54839
ISBN 0-8144-5589-1

First Printing

Preface

FOR the past twenty years we have worked as a family counseling team with managers who encounter troubles in their private life. More and more we see that the center of difficulty for these people is that point at which their professional ambitions impinge on their plans for private existence. Since most of the people with whom we were working were married to people who also had careers, we saw our own difficult choices between public career and private life reflected in their difficulties.

We wrote this book, then, as a result of practical experience. It is designed to demonstrate, with numerous specific examples, the crucial areas for people who are trying to balance two careers in one family. It is not a book for males or females, but a book about both. We have passed the stage where the woman stays home beside the stove while the husband goes out to bring home the bacon. And this new pattern has produced new problems that we have seen in our own marriage and those of others who have come to us for help over the years.

To avoid the confusion of strange pronoun patterns such as *his/her*, we have sometimes resorted to the conventional use of the masculine pronoun to refer to both. However, we want to protest here that the experiences recounted are for women managers as well as men. Sex discrimination in business has not disappeared, but great strides have been made, even if the language has not yet caught up with the changes. The examples here are equally pertinent for men and women, since both are involved in the complex business of integrating two careers into one family and two personalities into one marriage.

We do not deal in theories. We are managerial realists who derive any generalizations from numerous specific examples. We have not presented all the examples we have in our files, but we have given you enough to illustrate our basic points. Two-career couples have to be especially honest with each other about their aims in business and at home. This honesty has to take the form of continuous open discussion on the subjects that really matter.

To show you how this works, we have put our own experiences into dialogues at the conclusion of each chapter. You can take up where we leave off and join our conversation so that you and your partner can become more aware of the choices that are available to you. We believe that when you know the choices and talk to each other about them, you will derive a degree of satisfaction that will enrich all areas of your relationship—with each other at home and with your fellow managers at work.

William M. Jones and Ruth A. Jones

Contents

Two
Careers—
One
Marriage

1

Personal and Professional Choices

OUR personal lives and our careers are so interrelated that a decision in one usually influences the other. The choices we make exclude other possibilities and carry with them inevitable but often unforeseen consequences. We are all occasionally haunted by the suspicion that if we had been at a different place at a certain time everything would have worked out better for us. If we had made an A instead of a C in freshman chemistry, we might have been a rich physician today. When we consider such missed opportunities, we are likely to experience self-pity, guilt, or nagging frustration. These negative emotions may then blind us to another path we ought to choose.

This book is for men and women in management, people who can make intelligent administrative decisions but who are less confident in their personal and professional interactions. The case histories collected here will help you see how others handle the choices that most of us have to make when we are participating members of two-career families.

THE SAFE EXTREMES

People who are totally career-oriented or totally home-oriented are less likely to feel frustrated than those of us who devote ourselves to two worlds. These "extremists," because they give 100 percent commitment to one kind of activity, are not constantly forced to balance their public responsibilities against their private ones. Their universe has a unity that our balancing act sometimes lacks.

Laura, for example, decided in high school that she was going to make it big in business. She married a banker and immediately began selling real estate. When her children were small, she turned them over to a babysitter and spent her time showing houses until she had enough experience and capital to start her own firm. Before she was forty, she had branch offices in seven neighboring cities.

As Laura delighted in telling people, she took care of her business and her family took care of itself. When her oldest son asked her if he could go away to college, she replied, "Don't be silly! You know I put my extra money back into the business. You can start selling for me anytime you want to, though."

Laura's strength was what her associates called her "total professionalism." She never doubted the importance of what she was doing and never permitted any other choice—friendship, marriage, children, entertainment—to divert her attention. She became a legendary figure in her state. She addressed real estate conventions, lobbied for favorable housing codes, and enjoyed the admiration and fear of her business acquaintances. When her husband ran off with another woman, she told a client who happened to be in the office when she opened the good-bye letter, "I hope he gets a good job soon. I can use the alimony to open another branch."

Bruce was the opposite extreme—someone who chose the totally private existence. When he came back from Vietnam, he had no interest in returning to the engineering firm where he had spent his days at a drafting board before the draft board drafted him. He moved to a shack in the Colorado mountains and spent his time playing with his two children and fishing. His wife, Nancy, got a job teaching in a rural school. When Nancy came home from work, Bruce had the house clean and a good supper waiting for her. They had very little money, but they were satisfied with the choice they had made.

Bruce removed himself from the world of management, and this book is therefore not written for or about him. His 100 percent commitment to the private world saved him from the conflicts that arise when people have to make a choice between public and private existence. Nancy, on the other hand, continued to feel the strain that most people feel when they have to split themselves between the demands of their profession and those of their home.

Bruce and Nancy's agreement on their marriage roles led to individual specialization, with Nancy the professional person and Bruce the private one. For them, the arrangement has led to a fairly stable, tension-free existence. For the rest of us—two-career couples—our responsibilities to our family and to our profession require continuous compromises. We are happiest in both areas when we know what choices are available and learn to make them so that we are free of vain regret.

THE MODERATE MASSES

We asked a famous tax lawyer, who had not married until he was forty, if his marriage had helped or hindered his career. He did not hesitate a moment before replying, "Hindered it, of course." He went on to explain that he consciously allotted part of the time he had previously spent on his career to his new family. "The decision was mine," he concluded. "I made it gladly."

In his rational way this man had anticipated the demands of a family and accepted them as a part of the healthy mix that makes for a full life. With his characteristic clarity of vision, he planned percentages of invested time so that he could continue to control his career while putting time into his marriage as well. Even though we may not be as temperamentally cool about choices as this man is, we can become more confident of our choices if we are alert to possibilities and their consequences. The wretched people are those who blunder through their careers without being certain of the reasons they make decisions. One person blames his job for the collapse of his family; another blames his family for his failure at work. Both of them feel their lives are out of control; they are hanging on to a roller coaster that dips and curves unexpectedly.

As we know from our experience in management, every decision involves several choices. Some of these lead to favorable results, others to unfavorable ones. The more information we have about the situation, the more likely we are to come up with one of the satisfactory choices. The same kind of pattern exists in our daily decisions about our involvement in life—our relationships with fellow managers, our expenditure of time and energy. And the more we know about our aims and long-range goals, the wiser our choices are going to be.

We occasionally find ourselves thinking, "If I had only . . . ," but this fantasizing over neglected choices is unproductive unless it contributes to a better choice next time. By asking what it was that led us away from the accounting major we wish we had taken and to the last child we wish we had not had, we can sometimes save ourselves from similar unwise choices in the future.

Unless we accept responsibility for our earlier choices, we are likely to go on making poor ones in the future. Angela, who had a good job with a large insurance agency, noticed that several of the top executives in her company had master of business administration degrees. She decided she would get one too, so she enrolled in a difficult night school program that sapped her strength and enraged her with what, from her practical point of view, seemed to be useless theorizing.

Never doubting the value of the advanced degree for herself, she persisted semester after semester for four years. Her fatigue and the continuous stress made her difficult at work, so that she antagonized those around her and developed a reputation as a troublemaker. By the time she had her MBA she was wretched in her job and unable to get a good recommendation for another one. Bitter and resentful at the entire system, she continued to plug along at a job she had grown to hate, never realizing that she had made an initial unwise decision to expend so much energy on a degree that was not right for her at that time.

Responsible management of our personal choices requires more than an awareness of our own aims and abilities. We are also a part of a community of experience. Knowledge of other people's experiences can save us from making their unfortunate choices. If Angela had taken time out during her four arduous years to talk to her husband, her employer, or a good friend about her plans, she might have begun to suspect that it was a mistake to go on with the MBA. Her uncritical persistence dug her deeper and deeper into a defensive position that she refused to discuss or evaluate. Her personal conflicts arose from an unwise choice that she should have reconsidered periodically.

Angela's bad choice forced her into defensiveness and self-pity. Sometimes such a choice leads to an equally destructive sense of guilt that also spoils our ability to make wise future choices. Brent chose to marry right out of high school and immediately had several children. Once he made this choice, he compared his future possibilities with those of his fellow managers who had delayed marriage. Too late, he saw that his marriage was a handicap and grew both guilty and resentful because of it. Secret shame and a sense of inferiority separated him from his fellow managers.

Brent went back to school to try to improve his position. His wife took a dull, low-paying job to help with their expenses, thus adding to his guilt. Although he wanted a degree in finance, he settled for a teaching degree because it was quicker and easier to earn. He then spent ten years in teaching, resenting all the time his missed opportunities in business.

Poor early choices do not have to interfere with later ones as they did in Brent's career. Alone, we have no adequate models with which to compare our experiences. Advisers, wisely selected from our associates in business and personal life, can help us improve our future decision making.

GUILT AND RESPONSIBILITY

As we have seen, our future choices are often influenced by our attitude toward our past ones. If we are to be successful choosers, we must distinguish between guilt, which is a destructive force, and responsibility, which is a constructive one. If Brent, for example, wants to break his losing streak and free himself of guilt, he must make a responsible analysis of the decision-making process in the light of other people's experiences.

He needs to start by recognizing the finality of his past choices. Unless he is willing to surrender the responsibility of his wife and family, he cannot alter his initial choice. Accepting this present condition, he cannot act the way his single co-workers act. Anything he does is going to require more energy and money for him than for them. Accepting this condition, he can look back on his first choice and see that it was governed by a characteristic rashness, an impetuosity that is still part of his personality. By recognizing that trait, Brent can govern it and take his time to get the right training for the kind of position he wants.

Two-career marriages are cooperative ventures in which decisions work best when they are made by open consultations. When you accept realistically the current choices—balancing your personal emotional needs with your professional goals—you will be on the way to transforming undesirable guilt feelings into positive feelings of responsible family management. You can make use of your management experience by applying the techniques developed there to your private life. The partners in a two-career marriage often have conflicting aims and abilities, but frequent conferences, outside consultants, and research efforts will help you coordinate two careers in a single marriage.

The following chapters are designed to show you how other managers have coped with the presence of two careers in one marriage. These examples point out the co-existence of personal and professional demands, and show how they are best solved—through honest expression of expectations and cooperation in fulfilling them.

The Joneses Talk About Personal and Professional Choices

Bill: In our marriage how would you say we stack up as far as personal and professional balance goes?

Ruth: I think I've always put the home before my own profession. I haven't regretted that I devoted my principal energies to bringing up our children. At the same time, many women in my age group do feel that they have been denied professional fulfillment and are therefore less successful than the men and women who have devoted most of their efforts to professional success. It is a rare woman who doesn't feel guilty over lack of attention to either home *or* profession. Whichever one they're given major emphasis to, they feel guilty about the other one.

I think women have more guilt than men because their position in society is shifting so rapidly. Women need to make sure that they make rational and conscious choices and that they understand their motives.

Bill: You chose to work part time, and that means you subordinated your profession to mine. Still, the work you have done over the years has given you a professional standing in the community, and now that the children have grown you are profiting by returning to full-time professional activity.

I don't feel, though, that we've ever had a conflict. We pushed my profession because for the family it was likely to be the most financially rewarding. That isn't necessarily a male-related decision.

Ruth: The marriage partner who devotes less time to a profession— whichever sex—may find less professional gratification. On the other hand, he may just have less professional fatigue and bitterness. The main thing is to avoid being bitter about missed chances.

Bill: We've communicated well enough over the years to know that both of us have sacrificed for the marriage. I hope we've sacrificed equally. I think that we've considered each other's wishes along with professional necessity so that neither the profession nor the family has suffered. We've both always believed that the family came first. I've subordinated my profession to the family's welfare too, once in a while. Remember that big offer I turned down because of the local school situation?

Ruth: I hope you've never regretted that. I never have, but then why should I regret subordinating your profession?

Bill: If you were power-hungry or greedy for money, you might have. As for this, I think one reason we've made the choice we have is that we've never differed about our basic values. That's what I hope this book will do—help others establish or verbalize to each other the things that matter so that their choices, even if different from ours, will be as rewarding as ours have been.

2

Evaluating
Two-Career
Marriages

WHEN Charles married Esther, he said to her, "I want you to understand that this marriage must never interfere with my career." Esther, being very much in love, did not make the obvious reply, "And what about my career?" She recognized, young as she was, that Charles was simply expressing his insecurity about choosing to invest part of his time in marriage. Because of Esther's understanding and Charles' gradual acceptance of reality, they came to accept their marriage as a partnership in which they made their decisions for their common welfare rather than individually, as Charles had been thinking when he made his first ultimatum to Esther.

Everyone is not as fortunate as Charles and Esther. Many people find the balancing act between marriage and careers more than they can handle. Since the sex drive and the drive for power are closely related, we may confuse the two and demand emotional gratification from our job while trying to exercise power in our marriage. If we give all our attention to our career, as Charles threatened to do, the dissatisfaction generated by inadequate emotional gratification can spoil both our public and private life. On the other hand, when we neglect our career for our marriage, we can become so wretched in our job that the stress transfers to our private life and leads to such psychological problems as impotence or alcoholism.

Although at the beginning of his marriage Charles had an unrealistic attitude toward his future, he at least knew, in an inexperienced way, that he and Esther should agree on their public-private priorities. As long as both members of a couple agree on the nature of their marital partnership, they can adjust to adverse external pressures. The Macbeths are Shakespeare's example of "the happy couple." They agreed that ruling Scotland was more important than morality or sexual gratification. Even though their singleminded purpose brought them nothing but trouble, they never questioned their common goal—the kingdom.

Troubles arise when goals change after marriage, or when one member of a couple gives verbal assent to goals he does not support. To work well, marriage must be a rational, businesslike agreement. Falsifying emotional or professional goals to win someone's sexual favors is a sure way to plant the seeds of future job-home anguish. Esther took Charles on his own terms, hoping that his essential humanity would temper his professional drive. Esther took a chance and won, starting a career of her own to which she gave the same sincere commitment that Charles had expressed originally toward his. Far from interfering with their marriage, their professional commitments enriched it because Charles and Esther learned how to balance public and private choices to achieve their joint goals.

Millie and Jim were not as successful as Charles and Esther because they were not honest about their aims. When Millie married Jim, she was finishing up a degree in accounting. She planned to take a job with an accounting firm in Kansas City as soon as she got out of school. Jim listened to her excited talk about the chances for a woman in a big company and came to believe that they would make it together in the city.

By the time Millie began interviewing, Jim wanted to start a family. He convinced Millie that they should wait until the baby was born before they moved to the city. In the meantime they could both work in his father's business. His father needed a good accountant, and Millie would be able to do that job while she was pregnant.

After the baby was born, Jim and his family told Millie what a terrible place Kansas City was for bringing up a child. There was no need to run off to another town to find a job when Millie's father-in-law was glad to make a place for her in his business. He offered her a promotion, which she recognized for what it was—a bribe to stay with the family. Millie began to believe that she was ungrateful and thoughtless to put her professional ambition above the welfare of the family.

Under this kind of pressure, Millie became embittered and lazy. Never having had a chance to see if she could make it on her own, she spent more time partying and less time working. After several years of bickering with Jim and her in-laws, she divorced him. Their marriage could not stand the differences between their professional and private values. Jim, tied to his family and the family business, could not understand Millie's need for professional fulfillment in an independent world.

By permitting herself to be thwarted, Millie developed a resentment that was composed partly of guilt at her own weakness and partly of self-pity. Jim saw Millie's professional ambition as headstrong willfulness and irrational stubbornness even though she had told him what she wanted out of life before they married. With the added burden of constantly present relatives, Jim and Millie had little chance of working out a realistic compromise of their divergent professional goals.

MARRIAGE TYPES

Satisfactory maintenance of a marriage begins with the participants' honest evaluation of the type of marriage they have. From that realistic appraisal, the couple can then negotiate within that type or move toward some other type. Different personalities require different relationships. Although our own biases for one or another of the kinds of marriage discussed below may be evident, we honestly believe that people can be happy within any of these relationships. Both partners in the marriage, though, have to accept their roles and not permit peer pressure or media fads to make them question the essential value of what they have worked out within their marriage.

Liaison Marriage

The liaison marriage is, in a way, a contradiction in terms. A liaison is generally regarded as an extramarital, temporary sexual relationship. Here we are using the term to describe marriages in which one partner (usually the male) uses the other primarily to gratify his sexual needs. Although the sexually dominant member of such marriages may be professionally successful, he does not include his marriage partner in his professional life but treats the partner as an inferior object designed for his physical and emotional gratification.

This was the traditional frontier-type American marriage in which the male went out into the forest to hunt and clear while the female stayed at home cooking and having children. In their social life the women sat together gossiping over their quilting while the men drank and threw horseshoes.

As long as physical strength was necessary to subdue the public world, this pattern dominated. Now that shrewdness and intellectual acumen are replacing brute force, this conventional pattern of female subordination and male dominance is being questioned.

Cindy, in her marriage, has accepted the achiever role and tends to view her husband as a luxury. She works as a supervisor in a large hospital cafeteria. She admits, after some hesitation, that her husband is not working—"except on his motorcycles." She looks around somewhat guiltily as she continues: "He loves to play with his bikes. When I get off work, he's always waiting to take me home in the one with a sidecar. Then, after we eat, he takes me for a ride wherever I want to go."

Cindy has established for herself a liaison-type marriage with a man who is not reluctant to have his wife support him. She and he have no illusions about a future change in this arrangement. "I make the living," she says with a sly grin, "and he makes the living worthwhile." She has a good job and a man who satisfies her needs. When we asked her if she thought her marriage would last, she replied with a shrug of her shoulders, "Does anything?"

We would be less shocked at this kind of marriage if the sexes were reversed. Many executives have wives they keep in hiding, wives whose backgrounds or inclinations make them unsuitable for display at corporate entertainments. These executives find it best to put their public and private lives in widely separated compartments. If asked, they will say, "Yes. I'm married." But the marriage partner is a totally private person.

Most liaison marriages are extremely stable. They last as long as both partners are satisfied. Occasionally, the frustration of the separation of public and private existence causes tensions, especially when the working member is promoted to upper management. There, where competitors are using the energy of professionally oriented marriage partners to back up their own drive, the person with the totally private partner is at a decided disadvantage. In such situations, the professional life tends to absorb the private one so that the tensions of the career reverberate in all aspects of the marriage.

Mrs. Potts, who has built herself a sizable media consulting firm, flung into a staff meeting one morning and began lashing out at her staff in an irresponsible way. At lunch she was still seething. "Those people are stupid," she said. "They have no more sense than my husband."

Her luncheon companion, who had been at the meeting, asked her why she compared her staff to her husband. As her basic intelligence overcame her anger, she laughed and said, "Because I was transferring my irritation at my husband to my staff. Last night I went home to find the living room carpet on the porch and all the furniture piled in our bedroom. Ed was going to surprise me with a new carpet. And he knows how I hate surprises."

"You mean he chooses your carpeting without asking your opinion?"

"Sure. I don't care about things around the house. All I ask is that Ed keep things peaceful while I make the money."

For Mrs. Potts, her husband's duties are those of "homemaker." While she gives full time to her career, she expects her husband, who makes a feeble effort to sell real estate, to perform the private duties that a marriage requires.

This dichotomy of public and private function in liaison marriages leads to distinctive personality differentiation. The public professional, like Mrs. Potts, develops a strong sense of competition and aggressiveness that transfers to the private world. The nonpublic backup figure—in this case a male—gradually acquires the traits of a peacemaker. He is a passive compromiser, desirous to please, and sometimes so eager that his loving efforts act as a stimulus for the release of tensions that naturally build up in a careerist.

Mrs. Potts' husband, and Cindy's, would be shocked to think that they have a great deal in common with the kept women of rich Victorian businessmen, but their roles are similar. They are emotionally and financially dependent on the 100 percent professional with whom they live. And an awareness of that dependence gives them a timidity that encourages the more flashy public member of the team to enjoy a certain power game, chasing them around an emotional merry-go-round from which they see no escape.

Although we have used two female examples here to illustrate the prevalence of the liaison marriage, in the preponderance of such marriages the female is still the passive lovenest figure, dependent and fearful of losing her lover's approval. Even in a working couple, the female, who often makes less than the male—and whom society has conditioned to fear desertion and solitary existence—often continues to accept the passive role with gratitude.

The great danger in this kind of marriage, of course, is a shifting perception of dominant-passive roles. The subservient woman, seeing careerwomen of a different type portrayed in the mass media, begins to question her position. She, more often than a man in the same situation, is likely to grow restive and resentful. The men who accept this role are, for the most part, immune to majority social pressures and can stand up better in their maverick role of the pampered beloved.

Liaison marriages are clearly marriages of differentiated function, with the implication, usually, that the public function is more important than the private one. Even though the field-ranging member may reassure the lovenest figure of how important that role is, both usually give priority to the wage-earning position. And when two salaries are involved, the partner with the larger salary receives preferential treatment. If Jeff makes $27,000 a year as an agency chief and his wife Liz makes $13,000 in another agency, they use an economic yardstick to determine private responsibilities. Liz is the one who puts the children to bed, cooks supper, brings Jeff the paper. Thus this liaison marriage perpetuates the lengthy tradition of a warm fireside for the successful adventurer.

Marriage of State

In a state marriage two equal public figures are united and share joint responsibility for their public duties. Even though the woman may have been only a Bohemian princess and the man the king of England, once they are married they are accorded the same amount of ceremony and are legally joint tenants of the realm.

Although this analogy cannot be applied detail by detail to a two-career marriage of state, the general pattern is the same. In this type of marriage, both partners share equal responsibility in the public and private realms. Even though one member may earn a higher salary than the other, the two agree that their public functions will always receive higher priority than their private ones.

This kind of marriage is common in government, where the idea of bureaucratic necessity is strong. Nancy is a research specialist at the National Cancer Institute, and her husband, Greg, is a librarian at the Library of Congress. Although Greg's salary is twice Nancy's, it is generally understood that if one of the cars doesn't work Greg catches the bus and arrives late so that Nancy can have the car and get to work on time. Since Greg gets off half an hour before Nancy, he shops on the way home and starts supper. Nancy, on the other hand, handles Greg's official entertaining as well as her own.

When we asked Greg and Nancy how they determined individual responsibility in their marriage, they looked at each other in surprise, as if they hadn't thought about it before. "I guess we do what seems most convenient," Nancy said. "We don't discuss it much. We just do what we can to stay on top of our jobs. If he's got a heavy load, I take over something."

"And if you've both got heavy loads?"

Greg laughed. "We let the garbage pile up in the kitchen and eat out."

Then we asked the crucial question. We have discovered that you can almost always classify marriages by who makes the bed. In the liaison marriage the passive member always makes the bed as part of his private responsibility. Mrs. Potts, for example, was shocked that anyone would assume she had time in the morning to do the bed when her husband was around the house most of the day. He could do it when he got around to it. She had to get to the office, to schedule appointments, etc.

"Who makes the bed?" Nancy and Greg repeated. Then they answered simultaneously, "I do."

"Both of you make it?"

"Sure," Greg said. "We have a king-size bed that's hard to make.

Since we get up at the same time, we make it together. Nancy does her side; I do mine."

"It's the same changing the sheets," Nancy said. "They're too big to handle alone, so we do it together."

"When it gets done," Greg added.

This pattern, we have discovered, is typical of the state marriage. Since both partners place their careers first, they tend to treat the daily family responsibilities as secondary. If the bed doesn't get changed, they don't care. If the garbage piles up under the sink, who notices? They clean when their parents come for a visit because they know that it matters to them, but at other times the cleaning can wait.

In spite of the accord we found in Greg and Nancy's marriage, state marriages sometimes have difficulties. The utter faith that both partners place in their careers can lead to competition that affects every area of the marriage. Two ambitious people may strive for supremacy over each other, just as they do over outsiders. In Nancy and Greg's case, their respect for each other's career made them sympathetic and helpful. In other cases, professional pride can lead to destructive competition or resentment.

Even when the competition is not overt, external professional conflicts can sometimes harm the marriage. Sue, who had a new Ph.D. in anthropology, married Ron, who was finishing his law degree. "It will work out nicely," she said. "We're two professionals who respect each other."

"Sure," Ron added. "I can practice wherever Sue finds a job. Every town can absorb another good lawyer."

Sue took a museum appointment in an urban area, and Ron began working as a junior member of a large law firm. After several years Sue was offered a chance to do what she had always wanted—spend a year with an Indian tribe in western Canada. "Not much chance to practice law out there," Ron said wryly. "I'll wait here for you to come back."

"It's only for a year," Sue said. "I'll be back to my old job in the museum."

During the year he spent alone, Ron put all his energy into his work and advanced so rapidly that he was offered a partnership. Sue, free of any private responsibilities, was so successful in her job with the Indians that the Canadian government offered her an exciting field position. Having married without a realistic anticipation of their professional growth, they now found that the marriage was a handicap to their advancement. Ron did not want to go to Canada, and Sue liked her new job.

Like the two 100 percent professionals they were, Ron and Sue decided to go their own ways. Later Sue married a co-worker and Ron married a secretary in the law firm. Their second marriages, like their first, were state marriages. This time, though, because they had established themselves solidly in a profession, their marriages were successful.

State marriages work best for mature people who hold the same professional values. Sue and Ron made a false assumption to begin with—that Ron could practice anywhere. When that assumption collapsed, the marriage collapsed with it. Their uncompromising professionalism kept them from sacrificing good possibilities for advancement in order to ensure the continuation of their marriage.

Morganatic Marriage

Traditionally, a morganatic marriage is one arranged between a member of royalty and someone of lower station. In exchange for certain guaranteed rewards, the inferior surrenders all right to succession. As practiced in modern executive circles, this marriage is a combination of the liaison and state marriages. Like the state marriage, it is contracted between two professionals; but, like the liaison marriage, one of the partners agrees to take second place.

Jeb was a young neurosurgeon who fell in love with Angie, a surgical nurse working with him. They talked about the same things, knew the same people, shared the same professional world. It was natural for them to take to each other from the start. She admired him immensely, and he liked being admired. According to Angie, his proposal went something like this: "You're one of the best nurses I've ever worked with. You're intelligent, understanding, and responsive to my every need. Will you marry me?"

Angie knew from the start that her role in the marriage was to be chief assistant to the ruler. She accepted it willingly. Her admiration for Jeb's skill made their marriage a continuation of the relationship originally established in the operating room. Needless to say, we did not ask them who made the bed.

In the marriage Angie's professional pride at being the surgeon's wife offset any sense of inferiority she might have had. In her own functional unit—the hospital—she derived all the glory she wanted through her husband. She was "Mrs. Doctor Scott." Her power needs were satisfied by this kind of vicarious splendor.

Often morganatic marriages succeed because they are restricted to a closed circle of people with the same values. Neurosurgeons are accorded reigning privileges; and when they fight, they fight with other surgeons—a battle of titans. The little folk watch in awe. Occasionally, though, the inferior careerist in a morganatic marriage develops a sense of spiritual bondage that makes him unattractive to the ruler who admired him to begin with.

Carl, for example, was a hardworking insurance agent who found favor in the eyes of Robin, the only woman partner in the firm. She had inherited her place on the board from her first husband, who had been president. Carl's youthful vigor and devotion to insurance made him attractive to Robin, who was fifteen years older than he. She found special assignments for him, assignments in which she could be involved. She arranged for him to go to a convention with her in San Francisco. By the time they came home, they were engaged. Robin told her friends that what she admired was Carl's independence and ambition. "He's just like Lewis was twenty years ago," she said.

What Robin forgot was that she was not just the way she had been twenty years before. Carl was intimidated by her position and her experience. He married her because in a strange way he admired her and feared her at the same time. He knew that she wanted to marry him and, feeling the power of her position, he could see nothing but his own good fortune at marrying his boss.

Although they were both interested in insurance, they were interested at different levels. Carl still had to sell policies to make a living, and Robin had a theoretical view from the top. She found his industry petty and was hard put not to sneer at his efforts. They both knew that Robin was the leader and Carl the follower.

Carl's position at the office was an ambiguous one. His fellow agents treated him with new respect but also smiled at him a little behind his back. His professionalism was all that he had ever had, and now that seemed to have turned sour for him with his marriage. He knew from the beginning what Robin's position was—and what his had to be in relation to it—but his inexperience made it impossible for him to see the consequences.

For her part, Robin rapidly became disgusted with Carl's fearful fawning. "Why don't you show the independence you had when I first knew you?" she asked him. Yet, when he tried to stand up to her, she immediately pulled rank to put him back in his place again. Carl soon found out that the disadvantages of being married to the boss far outweighed the advantages. Unfortunately, he could not turn back on his decision, since Robin had control over his job. If he left Robin, he left everything he had worked to achieve. When he asked guardedly about a position with a rival company, he was told that the firm could not possibly offer him what he had where he was. Trapped, he was not a very good salesman or a very good husband either. His marriage dragged on, because neither he nor Robin saw an alternative to what they had arranged for themselves.

Angie's marriage to Jeb was successful because she knew what a morganatic settlement entails; Robin and Carl did not. Angie happily submitted to someone she accepted as her superior. Carl and Robin's unrealistic expectations were not a part of their marriage agreement and therefore caused them years of strife.

Love Match

In the three types of marriage that we have discussed so far, the career comes first in the relationship. In the liaison marriage, the active careerist is dominant. In the state marriage, the joint careers take priority, and in the morganatic marriage superiority is determined by professional position. In the love match, personal emotions are stronger than career drive. Both participants are inclined to place nonprofessional values such as love, honor, and each other's happiness above their career advancement.

The love match is the kind of marriage portrayed so often in popular literature and the movies. When two-career couples place other things before their careers, though, their careers frequently show the results of that slight. Laurie and Al dated all through college. Neither of them was especially interested in anything but getting married. They mooned their way through Love Story and The Other Side of the Mountain. As soon as they graduated, they got married. Laurie took a job as an assistant buyer with a large department store, and Al became an assistant manager at J. C. Penney's. They continued to go to the movies a lot and to eat out in romantic places, sometimes alone and sometimes with friends from work. They planned their vacations together and went to exciting places they had read about—Acapulco, Hawaii, the Bahamas. Everyone said they were the perfect pair.

After several years they decided they should have a child to per-petuate their love. Laurie took a leave from her job, but when she went back to work she did not have the energy or the interest that she had before. Al helped her with the baby as much as he could, but they were both tired most of the time. They gave up going out with their friends because they felt they should help each other around the house.

At work, Laurie started begging off from going on buying trips because she did not want to leave Al with all the work at home. Al, unable to compete with his more energetic peers, found that he was twice passed over for promotion to store manager. He and Laurie began making excuses for their professional failures. "We know what's important. It's each other and the family," they said. "Our jobs are only a way of supporting ourselves so that we can enjoy life."

But life was not particularly enjoyable. They never seemed to have enough money, and they left work undone when they finally dragged themselves to bed. In an effort to take some of the burden off Al, Laurie gave up her job and stayed at home with the child. Now they had no money at all for movies and eating out. They lost track of the friends they had known early in their marriage. "We have each other and the baby," Laurie said to Al. "That's what's really important."

By the time they put the child in nursery school, Laurie decided to go back to work. The only job she could find was part-time work as a salesclerk in a department store. Al grew discouraged with the drudgery of his junior position and shifted to another store; but younger men were over him, and he felt he knew more than they did. He was not easy to work with, and his salary showed it.

Al and Laurie still loved each other, but they were tired and disappointed because their professional lives were not satisfying to them. Financially, they were unable to have the kind of life they wanted, and the knowledge that they were smarter than the jobs they were stuck with sapped their pride.

As charming as a love match may seem, it is fraught with the dangers of idealistic romanticism that cannot stand up under continuous bom-bardment from reality. The love match may turn out to be a love loss for the couple unless they see clearly what the spurning of their professional responsibilities can lead to.

Personal pleasure is inextricably bound with professional success. By making short-term concessions to their emotional preferences, Al and Laurie found themselves in a professional bind from which they could not escape. Poverty may seem romantic in *La Bohème*, but in prosperous middle-class America it is hard soil for love to flourish in. Unless both members of the love match are realistic about the possible consequences of making choices strictly on a personal level, they are likely to find their relationship filled with bitter disappointment.

The love match works well when neither lover is ambitious for success or riches. It works even better when a safe job and an independent income make the luxury a realistic possibility. Professional people who find havens in a bureaucratic corner can hide for years. They are safe little cogs in the complex corporate machine. These unambitious types are useful to an organization partly because they are not ambitious. By putting in their time from nine to five, they pose no threat to anyone. After giving the company their forty years, they have the rest of their lives to spend with each other, enjoying the love match they have assigned top priority.

Magnetized Marriage

Many two-career families find that the magnetized marriage works best for achieving a stable relationship. Just as magnetized metal swings toward the North Pole, so a couple permanently charged to each other's needs constantly move toward each other. Like the points of a compass, they move freely around the entire circumference of human experience, but they gradually swing back to the positive pole—the other person. Those involved in the magnetized relationship know that while the other member of the couple is giving twenty hours a day to a business project, the pull within will bring his total attention back again when the sweep of the needle is complete. Even though he is absorbed in one activity, he is programmed by memory and emotion to respond to his partner's private needs. In a magnetized marriage, each partner is totally devoted to the marriage and totally devoted to the job at the same time.

The partners in a magnetized marriage do not consciously make sacrifices for their private pleasure. Decisions are always based on their own merits rather than on tangential, subjective matters that befog the real issues. People in a love match, for example, sometimes have difficulty making a private decision as simple as what movie to see. Al wants to see John Wayne, and Laurie wants to see him too. Neither will admit the preference, though, because Al *thinks* Laurie wants to see a musical and Laurie *thinks* Al wants to see a monster show. They talk at great length about which one they'd rather see, but neither will say because each knows the other will agree to that one too. They end up at a movie neither wants to see, missing John Wayne because they are making their decision out of self-sacrifice.

In the magnetized marriage such unnecessary selflessness is avoided. Each partner willingly states his preference from the beginning, knowing that the decision can be made only after they focus clearly on the possibilities. Then, in a reasonable fashion, they reach an agreement that is satisfactory to both. Maybe one selects the movie one time, the other the next time. The compromises are numerous, but at least money and time are not wasted on something neither partner wants.

In more significant matters of career and marriage selection, the same pattern works. The love match may lead eventually to guilt and blame: "If I hadn't put her wishes first, I'd be manager now." "If I hadn't been such a burden to her, she'd have a career of her own now." The magnetized relationship avoids such recriminations because each partner accepts individual responsibility for decisions that are jointly made.

Tim and Alice represent the way a permanently magnetized couple respond to new situations in their marriage. When Tim graduated from Haverford in 1959, his two older brothers told him he should go on to law school and follow the family tradition, but he was determined to live his own life. He took the kind of job he wanted with the kind of corporation he wanted and married Alice, the kind of woman he wanted. Neither he nor Alice ever had any serious doubts about the wisdom of their choices, even though Tim's older brothers were making big money and Alice's mother kept asking for the first fifteen years of the marriage why they weren't having children.

The success story continues until 1979, when it takes an unusual turn. Alice had always worked part time as a personnel officer for the telephone company. Eventually she moved to full time, earning a series of rapid promotions that brought her salary up past Tim's. Tim and Alice had always thought of her salary as a pleasant supplement to his. The dramatic increase in spending power put Tim and Alice into a new tax bracket and a new marital situation.

As Alice advanced, she took half the conversational time at dinner talking about people Tim didn't know and crises in which he was not concerned. Alice was developing an independent professional existence that made Tim see his own professional behavior in a new light. They joked lightheartedly about the reversal of the superior wage earner role, but Tim and Alice realized that—from their family tradition—they retained a basic assumption that the man was the wage earner and the woman the homemaker. Was Tim's self-worth diminished because Alice earned more than he did? Many of his friends and relatives would have thought so.

They solved their problem quickly by deciding not to tell anyone what their salaries were. To them, after the first whirling of their compass around the social-pressure field, they returned to the true pole—their permanent relationship. It was only their monetary positions that had changed, not any crucial part of their partnership.

CHANGE CONTROL

Sometimes we feel that we are on a treadmill going nowhere. That feeling occurs when we are no longer sure we are in control of our choices in life. Many of us have been married so long that we're hardly conscious of life before marriage. The same is true of our careers. We move from position to position, hoping the next will be more fun and more rewarding than the one we left. Still, we find that the future is more of the same thing as before.

Career and marriage should contribute to a pleasant existence. If they cease to do that for you, you can and should change them— suddenly or gradually, drastically or slightly, depending on your considered evaluation of your needs. The five types of marriage just discussed probably cover most of the executive marriages in America. Before you start moving toward one that is more to your liking, though, be sure you understand the one you have now.

We have a friend, a somewhat wretched spirit, who has been married four times. He keeps changing his marriage partner, but not his marriage relationship. Since he continues with a new partner in the same kind of marriage he had before, he is forced to relive his first marriage failure over and over again. If he could change the type of marriage to one more suited to his personality, he wouldn't have to change his partner.

An objective evaluation of your marriage-career relationship will help you draft a plan to bring about some constructive change without the trauma sometimes connected with changing partners. Evaluation is simply a matter of facing up—with your partner—to where you are and deciding if that is where you want to be in both your personal relationship and your career. Are you giving too much time to the private realm? To the public one? You are the only ones who know, and you are the only ones who can do anything to change it.

Suppose you discover that you are generally dissatisfied with your marriage. You look over the five kinds we've been talking about and decide that you are not ready for a drastic shift to another type. You can still do a great deal to improve your marriage, simply by considering the alternatives within that type.

If you are both satisfied with a love match, for example, you have no reason to experiment with something unsuited to your personalities. Be sure, though, that your relationship is genuinely satisfying, not something you think you *ought* to find satisfying. Often a frank discussion will indicate that one of you wants a love match while the other, down deep, would prefer a state marriage.

We said to start with that any kind of marriage will work if both members are satisfied with it. We add now that any kind of marriage will fail if one member is dissatisfied with it. Thus it is important that both you and your partner are living the kind of marriage you want to live. If you are, you can then begin working on rearranging the details.

That's what this book is about—the details. From here on, we examine those areas in which career and marriage interact to cause friction or peace, depending on the choices you have made so far. If you are feeling friction in any area of your marriage and are convinced that the basic pattern of the marriage is right for you, begin taking charge of your life and gaining control over the amount of change—and the kind—that is necessary to alleviate the friction.

EFFECTING CHANGE

It is not enough just to control change. You have to make it work for you, so that it contributes to a balance within the kind of marriage you have chosen. Looking back over the marriage types, you see that three of them place career first, one places the private relationship first, and the fifth tries to avoid making a split between public and private living. If your marriage is one in which career receives the primary attention—and assuming that is the way you want it to be—you may decide that you would like to sharpen your career opportunities. With that aim, you look at your marriage to see where you can find some personal time and energy to transfer to the career account.

Chad was forty-two and had been with the same company for fifteen years, the past six years in the same position. Beginning to feel middle-age inertia sapping his strength, he became unpleasant at home and began an affair with a thirty-year-old secretary who worked in his section. His wife Debbie soon found out, but she had seen enough middle-aged executives in her business to know what was wrong with Chad.

"You're not bored with your marriage," she told him. "You're bored with your job. Why don't you ask for a transfer to the West Coast?" When she told the story later, she admitted that her suggestion was not totally selfless. She knew the transfer would take care of Chad's career problem, but it would also end his affair with the secretary.

"I can't do that," Chad said. "I've got too much invested in this place."

"We can sell the house for what we've got in it and still make a little something," Debbie said. "What do you mean, you have so much invested?"

"I didn't mean the house. I meant the office. I've worked hard to get where I am."

Since Debbie was trying to be kind, she didn't ask, "Where's that?" Instead she said, "I have a job here that I like too, but I can start a new photography business on the coast. Nearly every town needs another photographer or two. What you mean is that you're afraid to start over again after forty."

They talked a lot longer, and it gradually became clear to Chad that Debbie was exactly right about his reason for not wanting a transfer. He was afraid. He hated his life the way it was. He was not even especially enjoying his affair, which was only a symptom of his general dissatisfaction with the way his life had turned out.

It was a mistake, his understanding wife told him, to think of things as having "turned out." After all, life wasn't over at forty-two.

Because Chad and Debbie's marriage was a healthy one of the magnetic sort, they talked through their difficulty to find that the marriage was on the rocks because of job dissatisfaction. By the time they had worked together to sell their house, ship their furniture to

California, and convince their children that life would not end if they moved, Chad felt young again. He began his new position with a vigor he had not had since he was twenty-five, and Debbie happily started over in her own career—but with several years of experience behind her and the encouragement of a grateful husband.

This is not to say that everything worked out well for Chad and Debbie simply because they moved to California. They still had their difficulties, but they were smart enough to know that they needed to define clearly the cause of their difficulties before they could begin to resolve them.

Once you have made an analysis of your marriage and determined the direction you want to take, you have to ask yourself exactly how much change your career can stand and how much change your marriage will take. Usually the area of your life that is causing you trouble will be the one least likely to withstand extra strain. Gradually, the weakness spreads to all areas, as it did with Chad when he got involved with the secretary. But his marriage was stronger than his job, so that it withstood the shift to a new position.

In other situations, the reverse pattern of change is preferable. At fifty-three Todd and Becky had built themselves a massive trucking company from a single truck that Todd's father used to drive. They had worked together so long that they regarded each other more as business associates than as husband and wife. Just as they were considering a merger that would gain them access to routes in five more states, their labor union launched a long and bitter strike. Becky developed menopausal symptoms and Todd became impotent.

All our examples can't be pleasant ones, and this is one of the unpleasant ones. Neither Becky nor Todd had the stamina left to go through a realistic analysis of their situation. They blamed each other for the impotence, the strike, the eventual failure of the merger. They divorced and entered lengthy litigation over control of the company.

It was easy for their friends to see what should have happened, but no one could talk to either of them. If they had not permitted themselves to become victims of change, they might have begun a program for effecting positive change. The analysis should have begun with the acceptance of their advancing age. The merger, which would have been a good thing when they were thirty-five, was too much of a strain for them in their fifties.

The advance of middle age and the strike could not have been changed, but Todd and Becky should have accepted them as an inevitable part of life to be isolated and dealt with. In this situation, unlike that of Chad and Debbie, the professional relationship dominated the marriage. Both these career people had given most of their attention for the past thirty years to the trucking company, so that their marriage became a backdrop for their professional activities.

They could have reestablished a balance between the two by decreasing the amount of time spent on their careers and putting that time into the marriage. They could have passed up the merger offer and said, "I think for the time being we have enough to handle. Let's keep the business the way it is." Then they could have focused their attention on union negotiations and improved working relations with the truckers. With the business in a stable condition, they could have put it in the hands of their competent manager and gone to Florida for two months.

Such a shoring up of their marriage would have eased Becky's menopause and cured Todd's impotence. But given the personalities of these two 100 percent professionals, it is no surprise that they made the wrong choices—choices that led them to lose control of both their business and their marriage.

Personal analysis can help couples like Becky and Todd see how they can become winners instead of losers in the change game. Here are three ways of effecting change, any or all of which may be necessary for successful control of the future.

Personal Adjustment

Change does not need to be in the outside world only. Often our evaluation concludes with the realization that external conditions have been harming us only because of our resistance to them. We then make an adjustment that brings us into harmony again. Becky and Todd, for example, should have seen that they had the ambitions of twenty-year-olds and the bodies of fifty-year-olds. Had they been willing to accept this physical truth, they might have accomplished far more at fifty than at twenty—but not in the same way. They did not change their approach to life as life changed them.

Changing ourselves to keep in step with reality is sometimes the only way to face the imbalance that arises between marriage and career. Yet many of us go on trying to be something we are not, long after we ought to know better. Personal adjustment sometimes means redefining our aims and controlling our wills so that we can handle the situation around us.

Joint Discussion

Adjustment to change often depends on the understanding and cooperation of others—usually the marriage partner, the children, the boss, or some group at work. Unless you are able to establish some joint discussion with these people, you are going to have little chance to adjust the situation so that it is in harmony with your personal and professional desires.

We once counseled Tina, who had been married to Fred for thirty-three years. For the past twenty she had been enraged with him most of the time. Our first question was "Have you two tried to talk this thing out?" Her response was "He won't listen to me." Fred's response to the same question was a wild rolling of the eyes, as if he were in great pain.

Tina had no wish for a joint discussion. She simply wanted to impose her will on Fred. She felt that almost since the day they married he had been more interested in his business than he was in her. They had a liaison marriage in which Tina existed primarily to fulfill Fred's sexual and physical needs. She knew no other kind of life, but she regarded Fred's job as her rival for his favors, and she felt it was cheating her out of her fair share of his affections.

Tina's response to the situation was a self-defeating whining that had gained her what she wanted as a child. She assumed the same technique would work to get her husband's affection and attention. With the whines were interspersed occasional shrieks, tantrums, and railing. No wonder Fred smiled with bitter amusement when we suggested that they talk things out.

Joint discussion requires that those involved listen as well as talk. The discussion should start with an agreement that all participants will make an effort to change if they hear a valid argument for change. Then, with the possibility of compromise laid open, a reasonable conversation can begin.

Often, of course, by the time you reach the point of joint discussion you have damaged communications with the other party so severely that it is not easy to be reasonable. When that happens, it is wise to use an intermediary for negotiation before you begin the major discussion—sort of a preliminary reaching out through neutral channels.

The pattern is the same whether it is within the family, as with Tina and Fred, or at work. If a co-worker is making you miserable at the office—and at home, where you carry your troubles like a briefcase—look around for someone, either a superior or a friend, who can initiate negotiations toward an amicable discussion.

Joint discussions are not foolproof. Some people will not be interested in peaceful coexistence and will make no effort to participate in a discussion. They thrive on wretchedness. With such people, at home or at the office, all you can hope for is a cold war in which you summon all your emotional strength to endure their irrationality. When the situation becomes unbearable you issue your ultimatum and go to war, knowing you may lose what little peace you now have.

Direct Demand

At times, neither a personal readjustment nor a reasonable joint discussion can bring about the change you need. At that point you have to assess your aim and decide if you want to use a more powerful weapon—the direct demand. At home it works this way. You find that you are staying up so late waiting for your seventeen-year-old to get home with the family car that you are not working efficiently. You know he needs a chance to run around with his friends; all the other kids his age stay out late in cars. But you still can't get your rest.

In a situation like this, where you are clearly in authority, the direct demand is often the best approach. You say, "I can't sleep with you out in the car. From now on you will have to be in at a reasonable hour." Then you determine a reasonable hour—from your point of view, not his.

Later your son may initiate efforts at joint discussion, using the other parent as a neutral source. Thus you need to make sure to start by establishing that your cause is a just one. You should not make a direct demand unless you are absolutely certain you are right. Your future depends on this particular arrangement—at least until someone comes up with an adequate alternative.

You should be prepared to back up your direct demand with a threat. Although you may not need to use it—or even allude to it—you should have it ready. With the seventeen-year-old the threat is implicit in the parent-child relationship. As a parent, you can take the car away, withhold his allowance, lock him out of the house, or take any other dire action if he does not go along with your demand.

The direct demand, backed by implicit threat, can also be valuable at the office. Either you have the superior power to use the direct demand, or you have some indirect power—through withholding a service from your superiors—to use it. Only a very clear understanding of where you are and what you are after will make the direct demand effective.

Assume that you are working eight hours a day and are taking work home every night. You know that what you are doing is essential, but that two people should be working on the job and the other person who is supposed to be doing it is letting you do it alone. When the situation threatens your home life, you simply confront the goof-off directly: "I've been doing this job long enough. I'm not taking any more work home." You don't add what is obvious. If your partner doesn't do his share, his job will no longer get done.

This direct demand for a change can work even between a junior partner and a senior one. You simply tell your senior partner that you have reached the limit and are going to have to cut down. Blame it on your spouse, your children, your physician, or your mother, but make it clear that the present conditions are intolerable. We've all heard about people who retire from jobs they've done singlehandedly to be replaced by three higher-paid managers. Those people have only themselves to blame. They might well have changed conditions sooner with a well-placed direct demand.

MASS MEDIA FADS

When we make a direct demand or initiate any kind of change, we must be sure that the change is something we truly want, not something we have been led to believe we want. We are products of our culture, but we need not be slaves to it. All of us are conditioned by the news we hear, the magazines we read, and the people we meet. If we really want more leisure time, fine. But if we have come to believe we should want leisure time, then we had better subscribe to another magazine or talk to a different friend.

Following the pack may be fine on unimportant matters, but on matters of significance we must be cautious, since we may be endangering a delicate home-career balance. Do we want extra work for more money, or do we want more leisure for less money? Do we really want the new position or is it only peer pressure that makes the competition attractive enough to keep our gaming instinct up?

Andy managed a suburban branch of the Valley Bank of Arizona. He had a staff of seven people, five of whom he had known for a long time. The families spent their evenings eating together, and everybody in the suburb liked Andy. He enjoyed his days at work and enjoyed coming home each night to his swimming pool and garden.

Then one year Andy went to the state bankers' convention and heard the keynote speaker talk about professional stagnation. Later discussion groups were held to explore the symptoms and the consequences. Andy's fellow bankers gave him looks that suggested his contentment was a symptom of the dread disease of the year. Andy came home convinced that he had a severe case. His days were wretched and he felt that he had been relegated to the provinces. He wanted a transfer downtown.

After a year of pushing and scheming, he took a subordinate position in the parent bank, where he knew no one and was in competition with everyone. He had no time for his old friends at the branch office, and in his desperation he requested a transfer back. But someone else had his old job, and he was stuck in a dead-end position with a salary that did not rise much beyond starting level. The next year he was not even invited to the state convention, where the speaker talked about midcareer burnout.

It is extremely unwise to base our expectations of any sort—marriage or career—on what others recommend. Marriage and career supplement each other and build on each other. Together they create a total life pattern that is more than either alone. While we recognize this larger view, we must also keep in mind that both are an essential part of life and any damage to one will diminish our total existence.

The Joneses Talk About Marriage Evaluation

Bill: Do you think we've made our readers see the importance of beginning with an evaluation of their marriage as it now stands?

Ruth: We've certainly reached down into our collection of cases to find those that demonstrate most clearly what can happen when the wires of marriage and career get crossed up. You almost invariably end up with a blown fuse.

Bill: Do we really do this kind of thing for ourselves, though? When was the last time we had a marriage evaluation session?

Ruth: I think we keep one going most of the time. Don't you remember when we counted that you had spent two and a half months one year giving training sessions to government agencies and the children were begging you not to go back anymore?

Bill: Yes. Without realizing what had happened I had let my out-of-town commitments creep up on me. I was spending more time away from home than the captain of a clipper ship.

Ruth: So we decided to get along with less money and more you. Even the children agreed they'd rather have you than a ten-speed bike.

Bill: That works very well for us, but do you think we have always agreed on the kind of marriage we have?

Ruth: I think our marriage evaluation took embryonic form on the boardinghouse steps at Northwestern. Don't you remember the letter from your mother with the catechism about how many children we were going to have, what church we were going to attend, what part of the country we were going to live in? You laughed and said the only important question had already been answered—"What is your view of the cosmos?"

Bill: Right. In our youthful way we had been talking about that for a year and finding that we agreed on practically everything. I think we were both revolutionists at the time.

Ruth: We were young, which is probably the same thing. We didn't have a place in society yet and I think we were probably afraid we never would.

Bill: And now the evaluation continues. As we grow older we seem to agree that you work harder and I take on more responsibilities around the house. This way you get a chance to know professional success, which has ceased to thrill me as much as it used to.

Ruth: People are lucky when they can vary their roles in marriage without varying their marriage partners. I think flexibility is the sign of healthiness in marriage, as it is in muscles.

Bill: Right. And the exercise people get at home transfers to the office, so that they don't crack when the pressures are on.

Ruth: I don't think we can overemphasize the importance of constant reappraisal of career and marriage roles.

3

Marriage Stages for Careerists

THE way we handle marriage-career problems at one stage in our lives may not work at some other stage. Remember how Todd and Becky, the trucking couple in the last chapter, tried to respond to life in their fifties in the same way they had done when they were twenty-five? Most of us make our operating decisions from previous successes and failures. If we tried it before and it worked, we'll try it again. A gambler knows, though, that only a fool keeps his chips on the same number every time. In the same way, we have to be alert to changing stages in our lives and the new choices that accompany them.

Although two-career families face some of the same problems as families with a single wage earner, they also encounter many unique difficulties. As we saw in the previous chapter, these problems are not specifically those of marriage or career but lie in the interaction between the two. All the couples we have seen so far would have made a mistake to blame their trouble on *only* the marriage or *only* the career. They would have made an equally serious mistake to blame only one member of the couple. If we are to handle the continuous conversation of life, we must work through joint discussion and joint resolution.

In any marriage people pass through stages. What you found boring or even contemptible at one stage you may find pleasurable and gratifying at another. What you once cherished, you now treat lightly. Take something as simple as office picnics. Harry says to Katherine, "There's nothing I despise as much as the annual office picnic. We go out to the park with people we work with all week, play ball like ten-year-olds until we're sweaty, and then eat dusty hamburgers and somebody's greasy potato salad. Why do we have to go?"

Ten years later, Harry says to Katherine, "They were thinking of doing away with the office picnic, so I said I'd serve as chairman of the food committee this year and try to keep it going. We can save it if we really work on it. I've asked the boss to serve as captain of one team and the board chairman to serve as captain of the other. Roping in the board this year was a great idea to give the picnic more prestige."

Katherine replies with a tired smile, "I thought you hated the office picnic."

Harry looks at her with surprise and says, "That must have been your first husband, dear. It's almost as much fun as the Christmas party."

Since Katherine's interests were changing too, she was sympathetic to Harry's reversal about the picnic. Their shifts kept their relationship interesting. It is the same for most of us who live in the two-pronged universe of work and home. When we think we understand someone .completely, have seen into his soul, he does something so uncharacteristic that we begin our study of him over again. Even more surprisingly, we discover the same thing about ourselves. Our needs and tastes change so imperceptibly that one day we're stunned at something we do or say.

As these changes occur, they can lead to trouble unless we recognize them for what they are and integrate them into our planning. Each period of our lives has its own patterns and problems. Seeing how others involved in a two-career existence are coping with their problems can help us make wiser choices ourselves.

FIRST FUSION

Before marriage we are single creatures giving a sizable portion of our lives to working for part of the day and devoting the rest of our time to personal pleasure. This solitary period of our lives is not idyllic, though. We spend a lot of time being lonely, being disappointed by human relationships, being frustrated at work and having nobody to complain to about it—nobody who really cares anyway.

What characterizes this single period of our lives is its self-centeredness. As we work our way free of our parents, we have to make adjustments to the larger world. As we begin our careers, we go through a period of experimentation. We learn whom to trust and whom to distrust, what to do with our leisure time, how to work effectively to get the most for the energy we expend. We establish reasonable patterns for eating and sleeping, and we develop agreeable patterns of social interchange.

For most of us, this period of experimentation does not last long. It is spent largely looking for someone with whom to share the eating, sleeping, and socializing—a partner to whose life we can fuse our own. We then begin another period of experimentation—this time in partnership. That adjustment can be fun, but it can also be disastrous, since the early phase of a career and marriage—like the early stage of a child's life—is delicate and easily damaged. A bad start on the joint experiment can permanently scar the relationship.

During first fusion we have to be willing to make some compromises to maintain the partnership. Something has to give if the fusion is going to work. Our solitary rest pattern, eating pattern, social pattern, and job pattern must now be integrated with someone else's. No matter how much we've planned and talked before marriage, when we move in with someone else we find a multitude of details to be dealt with.

We begin our marriages by deciding to do some things the way our parents did and swearing that we will never do other things that way. During first fusion we often say, "That's the way my mother used to do it," meaning "That's the way it ought to be done," and "I'll never make the mistake my parents made," meaning "That's got to go."

Forrest and Cora began dating in high school. They knew and liked each other's families. Only after their marriage did the differences in the two families begin to show up. Although both of Forrest's parents worked, the husband-wife lines were clearly drawn in the family. It was considered "sissy" for the man to be in the kitchen at all. Forrest's mother came home from work, cooked supper, did the dishes, cleaned the house, and ironed clothes while Forrest's father rested after his day's work. This standard lovenest pattern was sacred in Forrest's family.

Cora's parents had a state marriage, in which both partners shared equally in career and home life. If Cora's mother cooked the meal, her father cleaned up afterward. If her mother did the ironing, her father changed the beds.

For the first few weeks of their marriage Cora enjoyed cooking and cleaning up for Forrest, but she soon began to resent his inactivity around the house. The first time she asked him to help with the laundry, he put his feet up on the coffeetable, laughed, and said, "That's woman's work."

Cora had had a bad day with her boss and was angrier at Forrest than she should have been. She did the laundry herself but was silent and resentful the rest of the evening. The next day, when Forrest told her to get the car filled with gas, she didn't say anything. When she drove it home from work that night the tank was almost empty. "Why didn't you fill the tank this morning?" he asked. "You knew I was going out tonight."

"That's man's work," she said with tight lips and slammed the bedroom door.

Such traditional patterns of expectation can spoil the development of a loving, supportive fusion. Cora and Forrest made things worse by turning to their families for support. Forrest told his father the story of their first quarrel, and Cora told her mother. Forrest's father said, "You can't let her start getting away with such behavior. Whip her into shape." Cora's mother said, "Men are brutal sometimes. Be sweet, but don't give an inch."

Thus the battle lines were drawn. Actually, Cora and Forrest were a new generation with new work patterns and an opportunity to make their own life—working together to advance in the public world and working together to make a comfortable existence at home. People with divergent family backgrounds can create their own marriage type, but they have to be sure that they agree on what they want. Forrest wanted a male-dominated lovenest, and Cora wanted an equal place in the work-home relationship. Forrest had no experience with participation in home management and believed that he needed none. Cora felt that if she spent as much time at work as Forrest did, he should do as much work at home.

Many families do make the adjustment Cora and Forrest failed to make. Two families we know have made it successfully in quite different ways. In one family, the working wife is glad to possess the home completely. She accepts her double role as wage earner and homemaker. She is happy to have her husband stay out of *her* kitchen and utility area. If he ironed his own shirt, she would think that he no longer loved her. In the other family, the wife says to an agreeable husband, "I work half time; you do half the housework. I work full time; I do none of the housework."

Marriage patterns are best worked out in premarital discussions, but in our society the parents are often so eager to see their children married that they guide them toward marriage with hasty encouragement. "Don't worry!" they say. "Everything will work out after you're married because you love each other."

Love can grow or wither, depending on the amount of realistic discussion that takes place both before and after marriage. Knowing the types of marriage can help you see the adjustments others have made. And finding a type suited to your own personalities can help you through that first year of fusion.

As suggested earlier, marriage patterns in our society change from year to year; even within one type of marriage, the responsibilities sometimes change. Such temporary conditions as poor health, extra work, and extra duties at home can alter individual responsibilities. A flexible, understanding relationship makes these adjustments much easier. Here are some special problems that will need attention in any type of marriage.

Different Boiling Points

When Frances and Claude married, they had both been working in managerial jobs for about five years. Frances was an administrative assistant in a large department and supervised twelve secretaries.

Claude was foreman in a grocery supply company. In his eagerness to be helpful, Claude rushed home from work every night and started supper. When it was over, he jumped up and did the dishes. Gradually he took over the grocery shopping. Frances offered to do it, but Claude said, "No, since I do most of the cooking, I may as well buy the things for the kitchen. I know what we need better than you do."

Over the first year, Frances took less and less initiative around the house. Soon Claude was making the bed, doing the wash, and deciding when the windows needed cleaning. The results of Claude's eagerness showed up in their professional lives. Frances became less certain of her administrative decisions than she had been before marriage. She allowed office discipline to decline, and bickering began among her staff where there had been concord before. The passive, protected home life was reflected in Frances' job.

Claude, on the other hand, became demanding and overbearing with his crew. His behavior fostered resentment and discontent. The men felt that he was driving them too hard and was not as interested in their welfare as he had once been. With his own boss, Claude was sometimes slightly insolent and resentful. He felt he deserved more than he was getting. He was working harder and not receiving as much pleasure or reward for his effort.

At home a silent barrier gradually developed. Frances permitted Claude to do all the talking, and she listened with the same silent resentment that Claude noticed with his men. The two of them turned to outside friendships. Frances found the women at work more interesting and responsive than Claude. Claude enjoyed the people who worked for him, especially those who tried to curry his favor.

When Frances and Claude talked to us, we recognized right away that the problem was their "divergent boiling points." This phenomenon can be destructive in marriage and in associations at work unless it is recognized and controlled. Here is how it works.

In physics the boiling point is the temperature at which a substance begins to boil. The boiling point of water is not the same as that of mercury or lead. People too have a wide variety of boiling points. Claude's was much lower than Frances'. Consequently, he began to perk first. Naturally, she began to feel pushed aside. She said, "He makes me feel like a guest in my own house. He is so greedy that I can't do anything without him wanting to help me with it. So why should I try? He'll end up doing it anyway."

Claude, on the other hand, began to think that Frances was not doing her share. Initially, he had enjoyed doing things for her, and he thought he was doing her a favor to take some of the household burdens off her shoulders. As time passed, he began to feel the strain of total responsibility. She grew more passive, and he became more frantically aggressive. Neither of them recognized the cause of their conflict. They were conscious only of a constant irritation that made them want to get away from each other. Frances watched a lot of evening television, and Claude began going out for drinks with his unmarried friends.

If they had recognized their different boiling points, they might have divided their tasks at home so that they shared equally in running the household. Frances was a competent manager, but she was slower getting started than Claude. She felt that Claude might have taken more time with things and done a better job. Claude thought Frances was lazy. Neither was right. With loving understanding, they could have combined his eager energy and her careful craftsmanship to make their marriage a pleasure rather than an irritant.

Personal Identity

Frequently a woman merges her identity with her husband's, and, as she takes his name, so she assumes a dependent role in the relationship. In two-career families, this merger does not occur in the same way that it has in previous generations. Now women, especially working wives, are more likely to retain their personal identities.

Even an enlightened careerwoman, though, may encounter identity problems. She is still the same person she was before she married, but she has a new relationship that changes some of her previous patterns. The conventional pull toward conformity may make her anxious to accept the name of the man she loves and be bound to him in title as well as in law.

But the difficulties of this choice are immediately apparent. If she has a widespread professional reputation, she has to go through the awkwardness of a name change. Those who think of her as Carlotta Pike are going to have to remember that she is now Carlotta Sneed. If her name is part of her business, she may choose to establish two identities, one in her private life and another in her public life. If she decides not to change her name, though, society makes getting bank accounts and apartment leases a constant struggle.

The name choice, for a woman, is symbolic of more subtle decisions about personal identity during first fusion. Sometimes, when she relinquishes her single identity, a woman has trouble establishing a new one independent of her husband's. She is so absorbed into his world that her own professional sphere becomes dwarfed by his. Even when she retains her job, the marriage may give her a new casualness toward her work so that her performance suffers. She has another center for her life that takes precedence over her job. However, when she is the primary wage earner, for whatever reason, her work may improve with marriage. She has purpose and sparkle that enable her to face her superiors more confidently. She becomes more assertive in her dealings with equals and subordinates.

Whatever her relationship with her husband, her personal awareness may undergo stages of transformation that should be regarded as perfectly natural. In suppressing these changes she takes a chance on relinquishing her personal identity and merging it with her husband's. Even in a lovenest type of marriage, the woman who becomes only an extension of her husband loses her appeal rather quickly. As one husband said rather sadly, "She used to be more fun when she fought back."

The man's identity doesn't undergo the same kind of change as the woman's. His is in no danger, ordinarily, of being submerged. In his first fusion, though, he is sometimes frightened by his new responsibilities. He may feel a loss of independence that is psychologically threatening. He works harder, worries more, and sometimes responds violently to restrictions on his former pattern of existence.

Henry and Jana went through a typical first-fusion challenge to their personal identities. Henry was moving along well as a sales manager in his company when he married Jana. She had been working for five years—since high school—in the computer center of an insurance company. She had recently moved up to the position of night supervisor. After she married, she found the night work unsatisfactory and asked to be moved back to a lower-paying daytime position.

This decision was not forced on Jana. She freely chose to put her marriage before her career. She also readily agreed to Henry's suggestion that they live on his pay check and bank hers. Although the choices were reasonable ones, they shook Jana's confidence. She had always been ashamed that she had not gone to college; and now that she was being introduced to executives' wives, she was embarrassed to say that she worked in a computer center. Whenever she met Henry's friends, she would say somewhat defensively, "I was a supervisor before I married."

Because Jana felt a professional loss as a result of her marriage, she began to grow resentful of Henry. She responded to him with a combination of subservience and insolence, something like a saucy servant. She constantly found fault with Henry's behavior around the house. Why didn't he wear his shirt at the supper table? Had he no respect for her efforts in the kitchen? Couldn't he wipe his feet before he came in? He should not put a wet glass down on the coffeetable. Henry, who had admired Jana for her poise and independence, began to wonder what had become of the person he married. Neither of them recognized the symptoms of personality readjustment that are inevitable during first fusion.

Convinced she had to make some job change to accommodate herself to the marriage, Jana freely accepted a morganatic marriage in which her career was sacrificed. That shift was not, necessarily, a debasement. Jana could have seen it as a positive, valuable contribution to the marriage. She could have assumed important household responsibilities, such as management of the family finances, to replace her lost professional prestige. Instead she and Henry made a second decision to treat her earnings as unnecessary, thus further deemphasizing her importance in the marriage.

Jana's harping at Henry was a way of asserting the importance of her part of the marriage duties, but neither knew that. Henry simply drove himself to achieve more at work, and that only irritated Jana further. It never occurred to either of them that their first fusion, even though inadequately accomplished, was not their final choice. They could have made a new start at any time with renewed affection and understanding. As it was, they ground their lives away in a morganatic relationship that was not suited to either of their personalities.

Job Dissatisfaction

Frequently inadequate first fusion leads to job dissatisfaction, but the reverse is often true as well. Julie and Carey married while Carey was still in college getting a degree in journalism. Julie worked as a departmental secretary at the university. In her three years there she had developed good friendships with most of the members of the department and was regarded as exceptionally competent.

Carey finished his degree and took a position as a sports reporter on the local paper. Although he had majored in journalism, his real interest was in creative writing. He resented the hours he had to put in at sports events and the amount of supervision that the sports editor gave his writing. When Julie came home at night, eager to talk about her friends at the office, he found it difficult not to be envious of her happiness.

Carey's moodiness at home upset Julie, and she tried to find out what was wrong. At first Carey did not want to tell her, but gradually his dissatisfaction with his job became clear. "Why don't you try something else?" Julie suggested. "I make enough money for you to take a chance. Quit your job and just write for a while."

Carey went down to work the next day, had a big fight with his editor, and stormed out of the office. He came home and sat down in front of his typewriter, ready to produce the Great American Novel. But nothing much happened.

Julie was sympathetic again, but that just made it worse. Carey felt guilty that she had supported him for two years of college and was now doing it again. He went out and got a job as an insurance salesman because his blast at the sports editor had closed the door to newspaper work for him in that town. The competition for sales was fierce in the area, and Carey was not an aggressive salesman.

By the end of their first year of marriage, Carey felt trapped in a life that he did not want with responsibilities that he could not meet. In his desperation he resented Julie, who had never even asked for his gratitude. He squandered their money on beer for people he hardly knew in an effort to find friends. Julie gradually realized how hopeless their situation was and left Carey, not because she did not still love him but because she saw that his dissatisfaction was destroying their chances of happiness.

This case is not an extreme or unusual one. Job dissatisfaction can make either man or woman feel desperately trapped. The solution is not a quick rebellion, as with Carey's change of jobs, but a thoughtful investigation of realistic possibilities. Job dissatisfaction, coming as it often does at the time when first fusion has not been adequately achieved, threatens the basis of the marriage—loving communication. Since the two partners are still getting to know each other, they may not always make wise choices.

When Carey quit the reporting job, he was suffering not so much from an urge to write as from professional maladjustment. He did not accept the reality of discipline and authority. Coming to the job straight out of college, he found the routine burdensome and jumped at the first opportunity to get out of it. His guilt at Julie's continued sacrifice made him incapable of writing, and the insurance job was unsuited to his personality. Each shift of jobs, unless it is made with serious consideration of personal needs and abilities, intensifies job dissatisfaction, guilt, and the trapped feeling. Before Carey left the paper, he should have talked to experienced people who might have suggested some other field—advertising or editing—where he could use his professional training and still have more freedom than he had on the sports page.

Parental Differences

Parents are sometimes a threat to satisfactory first fusion. Perfectly happy, loving parents may become tyrannical in their effort to validate their own pattern of marriage by imposing it on their children. Wretched parents, on the other hand, may attempt to impose their bitter cynicism about marriage on the next generation.

Whether parents are sure their way is the only way or that any way is the wrong way, they can make first fusion difficult. We are dependent on our parents for emotional support, even when we are financially independent. Their disapproval is a severe strain on our marriage relationship. As we have already seen, conflicts arise when members of a couple come from different types of marriages. Some of these conflicts are the result of parental expectations passed on to the children. Even more are the result of parental disapproval of the new marriage pattern.

Pam and Chet's marriage illustrates how parental differences create problems. Pam's parents, Mr. and Mrs. Owens, had both worked since Pam was in grade school. They had invested wisely and still had money left over for a pleasant life. Mrs. Evans, Chet's mother, had given her life to Chet and his two brothers. She was the first to say that the only way to have a good family was to have a woman at home seeing to the comforts of the husband and children.

Mr. Evans had never made a lot of money, and he and his wife were resentful of two-career families that enjoyed extra income. Even before the marriage, the Owenses and the Evanses squared off for an antagonistic relationship. The Owenses were slightly condescending, and the Evanses were defensive about their way of life.

Knowing the differences between their parents, Chet and Pam still found it difficult to shape an existence independent of their parents. Pam kept her job after the marriage, but she was aware of her mother-in-law's scornful disapproval of a working woman and was therefore ill at ease around Mrs. Evans. Chet began to feel that he was not performing his duties as a husband because his wife was still working. But when he was with the Owenses, he felt Pam should continue working so they could accumulate extra money.

Pam saw that they were trying to please two sets of parents and were not pleasing anybody—even themselves. They talked the matter over and then made a rather drastic decision. They gave up their jobs and moved five hundred miles away to an urban center where Chet knew he could find work. Pam waited until Chet was comfortably settled in his job and then began to search the want-ads. She was bored at home alone all day and wanted something to do. Since she did not feel obliged to work, she took her time and found a job with interesting people and a good future.

When they wrote home, they were careful to suit their reports of success to their parents' respective prejudices. Some of the old tensions remained, but Chet had decided for himself that he was not going to be the kind of authoritarian father his had been, and Pam was free to choose whether to work or not.

Pam and Chet found that physical distance made it easier for them to be independent of their parents. Such a drastic move is not always wise or necessary. Living close to parents, though, requires conscious cultivation of your way of life. If you live in the same town as your parents, you must be frank and direct with them from the beginning. They have had their chance to live their lives, and they are not going to live yours too. You don't have to be unpleasant about your independence. Just smile pleasantly and agreeably when your parents make suggestions and continue to go your own way. If you are sure of what you want to do, you should not feel seriously threatened by parental advice or criticism.

The best way to develop confidence in your own way of life is to refuse to discuss your affairs with your parents. If you don't tell them what you are going to do until you have already done it, you will begin to experience the pleasure of choices freely made. When you make unwise choices, which you are certain to do, your parents will inevitably say, "I told you so." Again, just remember that they are simply trying to justify their own existence. Eventually your parental differences will fade away as you fuse into a family of your own.

MIDLIFE TENSION

The problems of the first years soon fade into insignificance. You have subdued your parents and your in-laws, overcome your dissatisfaction with your job, and established a personal identity suited to your marriage. You have also grown used to living with your partner and have worked out a relationship that is harmonious and rewarding. So what can happen now? New problems replace the old ones.

Most of these problems are the result of success, boredom, or disappointment. Realistic evaluation is the best way to solve these common midlife problems, just as it is the best way to solve the problems of first fusion. We are never either as bad or as good as we think we are, and unless we put ourselves in the middle rank of the world's successful executives, where we belong, our careers and personal lives are going to be less satisfactory than they ought to be.

Success

After a few years of vigorous effort you may approach the success you've wanted in your family and professional life. While you and your partner are struggling to get ahead, your common purpose keeps you close together. You drag home at night, tired but happy. You have a lot to talk about, and you encourage each other in hard times.

Then one day your bank account shows a surplus, you get a chance at the vacation you've dreamed about, and something begins to give in your work and your marriage. At work you look ahead to more years of the same thing. The competitive spirit flags. You wonder why you should work so hard to get any further when the top is so close. In short, a midcareer lull sets in. You feel the way you do after a European trip—jet lag has sapped your energy. You know you should be enjoying the fruits of your hard work, but the joy isn't there. Is it just that you're getting old?

Not really. You're suffering from a success syndrome that can be dangerous to your career as well as your marriage. First of all, let's look at your career. You may have grown dissatisfied with upper management and resentful of the restrictions placed on you. You are worth more than they realize, and you deserve more than you have been given. Success merges with greed—an inexhaustible appetite for more.

The greed is an outgrowth of your previous winning, but it can spoil future success unless you recognize it and control it. Resentment and power needs are best handled by channeling them into constructive new activities. Instead of becoming bitter, start an investment program, run for political office, or go in for free-lance consulting— anything to renew that sense of professional challenge. With a new project your resentment will disappear, and you will feel a surge of new power.

At the same time that you are beginning to experience success in your career, you may also begin feeling the backlash of success in your marriage. You may have children, a comfortable house, and parents and in-laws who have decided to let you run your own life. At this point the reaction we have already considered in your career develops in your home life. You feel that your partner isn't as sexually exciting as you would like. The same greed that threatened you at work now threatens your marriage. Your success drive makes you want to conquer someone else, probably someone who works for you or with you.

Along with this wandering eye comes a contempt for what you already have. You pursue the unavailable dream because you believe the available reality is permanent. Many successful people discover, however, that it is quite easily destroyed. After they destroy it, they wonder why they chose something they didn't have instead of cherishing what they had. Sexual roving, as we will see in the next chapter, is often related to success.

Boredom

Boredom can also lead to problems in midlife careers and marriages. You don't have to be successful to be bored. A stagnant, unchallenging job or marriage can also lead to boredom and can drive people to a series of destructive choices.

John and Irene married as soon as they graduated from high school. They worked hard and acquired enough money to open their own body shop, where they employed seven mechanics. John managed the shop and Irene kept the books and served as receptionist. Together they developed a sizable business. They liked the combination because Irene was able to take time off to have her two children and come back to her job when she was ready. They built themselves the house they had always wanted and in a few years saw their last child off to the first grade.

Then Irene began to feel bored. She had done nothing all her life but work, and here she was beginning to go gray, without ever having had any fun. She told John how she felt, and he decided they should take a vacation. As usual, he made the arrangements. He rented a trailer, and they drove down to a state park so he could fish. Irene sat around all day and cleaned his fish at night. After the third day, they had the biggest fight of their marriage—a result of success and boredom.

During Irene's solitary days in the trailer, she decided that she had worked as hard as John, but he got to make all the choices. She was tired of his smug, comfortable assurance. She was bored with his predictable responses to her efforts at conversation. She could repeat everything he said at any time of the day or night. The money they had made together was fine, but she did not look forward to doing the same thing for another twenty-five years.

By the time they got back from their vacation, John was extremely quiet and thoughtful. Irene felt sorry for him even while she was slashing at him in her boredom. Worse than that, she became regularly sarcastic with their son, who reminded her in so many ways of the man who was the symbol of her bondage. She cut him down every chance she got, so that John began to favor him. The marriage grew into an armed camp—Irene and her daughter allied against John and his son.

Irene carried her boredom to the shop too, where she instigated a secret revolution. She played up to the younger mechanics, becoming frighteningly sexy with some of them, so that they were embarrassed and nervous around her. With the older ones she employed more subtle tactics to turn them against each other and against John. She exerted her control so that the mechanics she favored were assigned easy jobs and the ones she disliked got the tough ones.

John's patience grew thin. In his goodhearted way he hated to see Irene unhappy, but he did not know how to be anything other than what he was. She had changed from the hardworking, ambitious woman he had married into an impossible shrew.

Irene and John's situation is characteristic of vigorous, successful people's midcareer boredom. Irene's bitterness toward her family and the breakdown of her relationship with John resulted from occupational and marital frustration. Irene and John had not cultivated a flexible, healthy atmosphere for change in their lives. They knew only one way to get ahead—hard work. When that was no longer necessary, they had no adequate replacement. John was willing to go on slaving in the shop, but Irene wanted new experiences and some tangible reward for the hard work she had put in. Finding pleasure in spending the money on vacations and clothes was not easy for her. She turned her view inward on the two areas of her life that seemed to be causing her boredom. The result was pain for her and those around her.

Irene's failure to meet midcareer success demonstrates two points. First, we need to plan for success as well as for failure. Second, when we recognize the symptoms of job or marriage fatigue, we should be ready with some positive remedies. Work alone is not enough to sustain a career, and home by itself is not enough to sustain a marriage. We need to give both regular vitamin supplements to keep them from becoming anemic.

Regular outside activities help keep the job attractive. During first fusion we work to get ahead, but unless we balance our work with leisure we will burn ourselves out. This balance is so important that a chapter is devoted to it later on. The person who drives himself deeper and deeper into work is likely to end up drinking too much, smoking too much, and dying too soon. Work has to be supplemented with an exercise program, social life, and constructive relaxation.

Marriage should be treated the same way. If your partner begins to seem dull or irritating, remember that it is decidedly easier to revitalize that partner than to trade for a new model. Vacations are fine if they are equally satisfactory to both of you. Even more important is developing a regular pattern of joint activity that brings you together under pleasant circumstances. Eating out is the kind of ordinary activity that can make you happy to be together and alleviate dullness. Any shared sport such as tennis or softball—or spectator sports, as long as you both enjoy them—can give your marriage the kick it used to have.

Shared pleasure is essential in both work and marriage. Make sure that you and your partner do not lose sight of what hard work is for—to enable you to have a good time together.

Disappointment

Whether we are successful or not, one of the hardest jobs in our middle years is coming to grips with our limitations, the ones that sometimes cause disappointments. These disappointments will shake our lives unless we control them. Once we accept the reality of changes in middle life, we are better able to face disappointment as well as success and boredom.

The owner of an expensive barber shop told Sharon, who was forty-one, that he was replacing her as manicurist because "the men like young women better." After her initial rage and disappointment, Sharon decided not to be defeated. From her years of observing customers who came into the shop, she decided that they liked class more than they liked young women. She borrowed money from one of her customers and opened a deluxe hairstyling salon with trim by appointment only; the business flourished. Thus Sharon turned her disappointment into success. She would have never dared try starting her own business as long as she had a secure job.

Disappointment is probably at least as frequent in marriage as it is at work. The children don't turn out the way we want them to, our partners grow fat or stray from the ranks of the faithful, our sex appeal diminishes. Not all disappointments can be turned to advantage, but they can help us focus on the present moment rather than on past conquests or future dreams.

Disappointments can also lead to a positive reevaluation of our lives. Why are we disappointed? Have our expectations been unrealistic? What can we do to make the present stronger and less vulnerable to disappointment than the past? By asking ourselves such questions we minimize disappointment and learn to tailor our expectations to our abilities.

When a disappointment comes along, we can weave it creatively into our future plans, knowing we will not try that particular road to failure again. We laugh the same way we do when we get off the elevator at the wrong floor. It's always possible to get back on and take the elevator to the right one—for us at that time. We may have spoiled a moment, but in the richess of time another moment is there to grasp.

If we keep our choice supply full, we can reduce midlife tensions to a minimum. They will occur, but they will be manageable because we retain the power to shape our own lives, even when disappointments come along. Despondency is the great danger in these years—that feeling of futility that can come with either success or failure. We can avoid that feeling by focusing on the present moment and culling from it what remains of promise and joy. If we look carefully, we can find quite a bit. Most of us are as capable of joy at forty-five as we are at twenty-five if we recognize our changed choices as promise rather than as threat.

DISCONNECTING

The day comes when our choices are not spread across a wide future, even though the present may still be pleasant. One of the toughest times of life for people who have been happy in their jobs and marriage is official retirement, an inevitable event over which we have no control. The power of positive selection still remains, though, even in this closing stage of our professional lives.

Until quite recently, people believed in the Doctrine of Plenitude. They observed that a flower makes a great many more seeds than are necessary to reproduce it, that a fish lays more eggs than could possibly be necessary to perpetuate the species, and that a tree has far more leaves than it needs to sustain its healthy state. They concluded, therefore, that the universe is a world of surplus materials—a Thanksgiving cornucopia overflowing with blessings.

We can see our lives in the same way. Even when we are denied an unlimited future, we have plenty to choose from—not the same things we've had in the past, perhaps, but numerous other things appropriate to our present age. We have a choice of relinquishing the past and enjoying present choices or of making ourselves unhappy by pining for what is gone. Like every other stage in life, we should face disconnecting long before we reach it. A great many couples act as if retirement was never going to come. They are invariably the ones who kick against it most painfully.

Marilyn, who had worked herself up to section manager in a large manufacturing company, knew that retirement at sixty-five was mandatory. Six months before her sixty-fifth birthday, her boss brought in a replacement to train with her. Marilyn made life so miserable for the replacement that she quit. Within a few months Marilyn had chased away two trainees and sat at her job smiling happily, certain the company couldn't get along without her. She was the only one patient enough and skillful enough to do her job.

A few weeks before her birthday, she received the standard retirement notice from the personnel office. She tore it up and began going around the office telling people that her boss had it in for her, that he was torturing her. She called people on the board of directors and told them that management was corrupt. She named two or three people who, she said, were milking the stockholders dry. In short, she flipped her lid. The company had to get a restraining order prohibiting Marilyn from coming back to the plant or from making threatening calls.

She sat at home all day. When her husband, who did not have to retire until seventy, came home in the evenings, she either railed at him or refused to speak to him. He still loved her, but she made life miserable. Shortly after her retirement, he had a heart attack.

The heart attack saved Marilyn. She was so interested in his diet and his recovery that she quit harassing her former employers. Suddenly she was indispensable at home in a way she had never been at the plant. That is what she found essential—to be needed. She soon made herself as unbearable to her husband's doctors as she had previously made herself at the plant. She accused them of not caring enough, of not knowing their business, of charging too much, but at least she finally made the transition to retirement. As she told her children, "It's a blessing I was able to quit work when I did. I don't know what your father would have done without me."

Marilyn's is an extreme case, but it illustrates the fact that we disconnect with almost as much effort as we fuse in the first place. Sometimes retirement is a physical strain. Ulcers, colitis, migraines, and asthma may not be totally psychosomatic, but they can sometimes be avoided by positive preparation for retirement.

It is easy to ridicule those who take a fanatical interest in gardening, oil painting, rug weaving, or fishing, but it is mentally healthy to have something besides work in our lives—even if it's just staying up late watching TV. Scorn is a destructive attitude because it keeps our future choices limited. We should try to have a few retired people in our circle by the time we're fifty so that we can see how they expand their private lives as their professional ones taper off. Here are a few methods that seem to work well.

A Natural Branching

The easiest way to disconnect is by reconnecting to a related area of activity. If we have spent our career learning about a particular subject, we can still use it even though we have officially disconnected.

Frank had worked as a farm appraiser for a large bank. He knew every farm in a fifty-square-mile area, who owned it, and how much it had last sold for. At retirement, he took his savings and invested in a farm of his own. His wife, who had also retired, thought he was crazy, but she was soon as enthusiastic as he was. They built a small house on one corner of the farm and moved in. They rented most of the land but kept a garden and some livestock of their own. The physical vigor of the life and the freedom from city traffic were just what they needed to give them new energy.

Many people who have been active in a corporation find that at retirement they are in a position to write up a history of their company, which the corporation itself may agree to publish. Other kinds of historiography are also valuable—histories of your college, your town, your church, or some social organization in which you have been active a long time. This type of writing offers you a chance to reorder the past and relive it in a pleasant, even profitable way.

Branching can sometimes be quite lucrative. Ross, whose job with the Securities and Exchange Commission prohibited him from trading in stocks and bonds, began investing at retirement. The accumulated knowledge of his career resulted in a new life for him. He continued his contacts with the people he knew on investment boards, and by the time he was seventy-five Ross had tripled his initial investment.

Like a tree, you have many branches extending from your main trunk. Even though you have given your position up, you can still be useful as a consultant for your firm or others. Your knowledge can also be valuable to your successors. A summary of office procedure or of recommended changes can make a lot of difference to people who lack your knowledge of past practices.

When you retire, you should stay away from your former professional environment until you are invited. You impair your usefulness if you get in the way after retirement. If you are distantly cooperative, though, you may develop a legendary status within a few years. People from the office will begin to tell stories about the time you pulled off this clever job or that one. So lie low, but remain visible by keeping up friendships and participation in profession-related activities.

Hobbies

Branching out can occur in areas other than professional ones. Sometimes a hobby that has never been a particularly important part of your life takes on new significance after retirement. We know one couple that played bridge casually most of their married life; when they retired it became their consuming passion. They joined a bridge club that played once a week and held informal practice sessions at other times. They went to international conventions and developed a sizable library of books on bridge.

You can branch out in areas as diverse as square dancing, camping, fishing, hunting, stamp collecting, chess, and gardening. Any activity that interested you while you were working can be expanded to fill the vacancy. While you're waiting for the time when you can spend as much time on your hobby as you please, keep your interest in nonprofessional activities alive.

Sports

Sixty-five or seventy is not too old for participation in sports if you have stayed in good physical condition over the years. We know several eighty-year-old joggers and one couple in their eighties who are still entering sailboat races—and winning. Sports contribute to longevity because of their salubrious effects on mental as well as physical health.

If you are physically limited, spectator sports can contribute to your retirement interest. When Flo was given early retirement because of a stroke, which left her partially paralyzed, she thought her life was over. Within a year, though, she had begun watching television sports. She knew every baseball and football player on the major teams, and pretty soon she began making arrangements with a senior citizens' group to go to the in-town games. She quoted batting averages and passes completed to the people who got in the habit of calling her to discuss the games. Following her natural interest, Flo developed small pools for the games so that other people's interest might be stimulated too. Before long she was supplementing her retirement income with her winnings.

Travel

Travel is a good way of disconnecting because it offers challenges and removes you from what you may have come to regard as the only world worth knowing. Even if you have traveled during your professional life, you may find other kinds of travel satisfying. Several of our friends have found travel very valuable, in quite different ways.

Otto spent most of his professional career traveling. He was a regional representative for a textbook publisher, and for forty years he drove all over the United States, first in the Midwest and later on the West Coast. After the children left home, his wife Ella quit her job and traveled with him. When he retired, they sold their large house, invested the profits, and moved into a small apartment. With the interest from their investment plus their retirement income, they spent three months a year in Italy. The rest of the year they read and planned their trip. In Italy they took a small villa in the countryside, rented a car, and explored what they had been reading about. When they came home, they developed their slides and gave lectures on Italian art and literature.

Ella and Otto had had enough domestic sightseeing before retirement, but foreign travel was a natural extension of their professional lives. Helen and Sam had been tied to a family heating business for thirty-five years. Their vacations consisted of visiting relatives—their parents first and then their children. Three years before they retired, they bought a condominium on the Atlantic coast and spent their vacations there, renting it out the rest of the year. By retirement time they were familiar with the place and enjoyed spending half the year there, in an area so attractive that their children look forward to coming to see them.

If you buy a retirement home in a place popular at other times of the year, you can spend two or three months there and make money on it when you aren't using it. One of our friends did quite well with a Vermont farmhouse, where he spent the summers while renting it to hunters and skiers during the winter. Another friend did the same with his Colorado cabin.

You don't have to make a large investment in a vacation home to enjoy extended travel. Some people are lucky enough to know those who need house sitters while they are away. With a little effort you might even make expenses by taking care of someone else's luxury beach cottage or mountain chalet.

One couple who had a relatively solitary existence during their professional lives wanted a wide circle of friends when they retired. They found an inexpensive resort on the Texas coast where people came back year after year. Living there gave them the same sense of permanence that they had had in their city home, but with a more congenial group. They look forward now to several winter months with "old friends" who fish, swim, play golf, and dance together.

Many parts of the country offer such economical alternate lifestyles. Arizona has its winter visitors who come in droves looking for companionship—nice people with good taste and good manners. Settlements of the same kind exist in California, Florida, Georgia, North Carolina, and South Carolina. Almost any area with an attractive climate or geography offers an excuse for congregating. Most of these areas offer a wide variety of housing so that you can find a place that will not stretch your retirement budget.

If you aren't ready to put in the time and effort on a second home or a regular vacation resort, you can still satisfy your travel urge by organized tours. Earl and Shelly, who had worked closely with people in their professional lives, felt lonely when they retired. Since most of the people they knew were still busy with their professional lives, they looked around for people with leisure and an eagerness to expand their private world. They signed up for a Caribbean cruise and came back with two couples who were planning to go to Europe with them the next fall.

There are any number of domestic tours that will take you to some part of the country that you've never seen. A bus tour of the West, a canal tour of the East Coast, or a steamboat junket down the Mississippi will throw you in with a group from which you can select compatible friends to correspond with or visit. A longer tour to Mexico, Canada, Europe, Asia, or Africa will unite you with other people through your shared experience. When you meet again on another tour, you have the previous one to talk about, other acquaintances to remember, and all the other amenities that make for warm, life-expanding relationships.

Another way of expanding your private world after retirement is through visits and visitors. Many people whom you haven't seen for years because you were busy with work are now in a position similar to your own. Start with a letter or phone call and see if you can't work out an invitation. Have them come to you, or go to them. You will often find that old friendships have not died but have simply gone dormant. If you liked certain people when you were eighteen or twenty, you may still like them—for the same reasons you did then.

Visits with relatives can also relieve loneliness, but you have to be sure you're not intruding. Younger relatives are busy getting ahead, the way you were in your own first fusion. Even with your children, it is best to keep the visits short. Remember how you felt at thirty when older people came to visit? You doubled up with the children to provide beds, cooked extra meals, and stayed up late to get the office work done. If you don't wear out your welcome, though, these short visits to children and grandchildren—and uncles and cousins—can be a good way to expand your private world.

Social Service

Sometimes developing an interest in others can help you make new connections and take your mind off your own professional change. When Ferd was sixty-five, he began going out three mornings a week to help with the sports program at a school for handicapped children. One child, who had never spoken a word, developed such an attachment to Ferd that he cried on the days Ferd didn't show up to play with him. The school psychologist felt that this indication of preference was a tremendous breakthrough for the boy.

Two years later, when Ferd's wife Carla retired, they both went out every morning to do volunteer work with the children. They demonstrated such a knack for handling problem cases that they were hired by the board as part-time employees. As Ferd said, "It doesn't seem right to be paid for doing something you love doing, but the money's nice too."

Not everyone is as lucky as Ferd and Carla. You may have to serve on several boards and try several volunteer groups before you find something that is appropriate for you. But the world of volunteer work is large. We know people whose time with hospital volunteer groups is so important that they will not even take a vacation because it would mean missed workdays.

You may have no choice about retirement, but you have a lot of ways to fill the professional gap, as you have seen. Let your natural interests and abilities lead you to an involvement that creates new connections. In determining your choices, you must know yourself. If you have always had lots of friends and activity, chances are that you will not be happy with a lonely existence in retirement. If you have spent most of your life engaged in pleasant, isolated work, you will probably be uncomfortable with a sudden shift to a frantic existence. Whatever you do, remember that in every stage of your career, from first fusion to disconnection, you want to keep open as many choices as possible.

The Joneses Talk About Marriage Stages

Ruth: If you were advising a couple just starting out, what would you tell them was the key to success at all stages of a two-career marriage?

Bill: I'd tell them, first of all, that it was probably very dangerous to oversimplify their thinking about two-career marriage. But if they persisted in wanting to know the key, I'd say flexibility is what they should cultivate at every stage of their lives.

Ruth: What do you mean by flexibility—giving in to each other and to circumstances? Bending under the burdens?

Bill: Not at all! It takes a strong-minded, purposeful couple to develop the kind of flexibility I'm talking about. Flexibility in a marriage is the ability to adjust realistically to those changes that are not in our control, changes such as growing old, getting sick, losing your hair. You know, the ones we have to accept.

Ruth: I see what you mean, but I think the pivotal word, along with flexibility, is control. Everyone needs to realize that many areas of life can be changed for the better. The flexibility you're talking about means not bending under the controllable things, but walking around them until you see a way out—the best way out. That's what we've been suggesting in this chapter—some alternatives to giving up when things seem out of control.

Bill: Right! Answers that were satisfactory at one stage are not necessarily so at another, but the same problem-solving attitude should endure the whole time.

Ruth: You're assuming, of course, that couples approach every problem in their career and their marriage with consistent, cool rationality. My experience, even with you, has been that at moments of crisis we're sometimes swept away by a wave of irrationality.

Bill: I know. But we shouldn't wait for the moment of crisis to train for that moment. Then it's too late to cultivate flexibility, purposefulness, or any other constructive trait. What we have to do then is just endure.

Ruth: Yes, but we endure better if we have trained beforehand. Surely there are some things we can remember to do, even in hysterical moments.

Bill: Are you suggesting that there are some rules of thumb to go by when reason falters?

Ruth: I certainly am. You and I have at least one that seems to work for us, even at moments of least emotional control. We always say to each other, when we see panic overtaking us, "Let's not make an irreversible decision until things calm down."

Bill: That's pretty basic. And we might also add, "Don't try to settle anything when you're angry or out of control."

Ruth: That's a safe one, but how do you know when you're out of control?

Bill: If you can't talk about something without your voice shaking, you're probably not calm enough to go on talking about it.

Ruth: Unfortunately, there are a lot of times when our voices shake, but I think our own previous experiences and those of other people we have known can help us through the shakes. The bad examples we've observed can protect us from unwise choices, and the good examples can give us courage to strive toward rationality again.

Bill: So we've concluded that controlled investigation of emotional situations is one of the characteristics of rationality. I guess that's a safe conclusion to this chapter, which has dealt with both positive and negative examples.

Ruth: Yes, as I look back over this chapter, I see that we have tried to collect enough models, good and bad, to see couples through some of the rough times. Other people's experience is sometimes the best teacher.

4

Sex,
Divorce,
and
Second
Marriage

CAREER differences in two-career
marriages can sometimes contribute to sexual problems. These difficulties arise when two-career couples fail to recognize the relationship
between their working schedule and their individual sexual needs.

Donna worked as an assistant manager in a branch bank. Her
husband Patrick sold business machines. Most of the week he was on
the road. When he came home on Friday night he wanted to snuggle
down with a beer and watch television. Donna, who had been home
alone all week, was ready to go out and celebrate. She was tired of
eating homecooked meals, and he was tired of eating restaurant food.

This career difference had a deleterious effect on their sex life.
Patrick felt it was his right on the weekends to have Donna cuddling

beside him at home. She felt it was her right to be treated to a good time. If Patrick took her out to supper and a show on Friday, he was usually too tired and irritated to be interested in sex when they got home. He would kick off his shoes, pile into bed in his underwear, and snooze away. If they stayed home, Donna was busy thinking about something she had to do around the house and was too resentful of her bondage to respond pleasantly to Patrick's advances.

These intelligent, otherwise successful people were unaware of the source of their growing sexual incompatibility. It increased to the point where Donna developed a headache whenever Patrick suggested sex, and Patrick was always too tired if Donna initiated an amorous scene. Their sexual maladjustment caused frequent quarrels and general dissatisfaction.

To alleviate her loneliness, Donna began eating out during the week with one of the young, unmarried tellers at the bank. Patrick began enjoying casual female company on the road. Both felt simultaneously guilty and resentful, so that the sex they found outside marriage was as destructive as that within their marriage. Having gone eagerly into marriage, they left it bitter and disillusioned. After an acrimonious divorce, they began second marriages that suffered from the same kind of maladjustment as their first.

PSYCHOSEXUAL PROBLEMS

The problems that Donna and Patrick encountered are not unique to two-career couples, but they are more frequent among them because both partners are more likely to expect private gratification. A good place to begin our study of working couples' sex-related marriage problems is with an analysis of where Patrick and Donna went wrong.

The sexual urge is a complex expression of personal instinct and social expectation. As social patterns change, sex sometimes undergoes painful readjustments. With Patrick and Donna, the central problem of their marriage was their *separate working patterns*. Tensions developing from this basic and permanent part of their married lives resulted in sexual incompatibility and the estrangement that such unsatisfied sexual needs generate.

Separate working patterns are a hindrance to sexual fulfillment only if we fail to recognize them for what they are. Patrick and Donna failed to see their central problem because most of their friends worked the same hours as their partners in similar kinds of jobs. Couples who are office-bound from nine to five develop similar tastes and after-hours needs. Thus, when Donna or Patrick talked to some of their friends about their marital difficulties, the friends did not understand the consequences of the separate working pattern.

In a marriage where only one person works, the separate working pattern is also present. The diversity is especially clear with a mother who stays at home and a father who works out of the house all week. In these situations, though, the homemaker tends to defer to the wage earner and adjust her schedule to his. She arranges her life to suit his needs by establishing a social world of her own while he is away. She has morning coffee in the neighborhood, plays bridge with other women, and satisfies her need for socializing during the day so that she can enjoy her husband when he comes home.

Patrick and Donna could have worked out some type of compromise if they had discussed their divergent needs. Donna, who wanted to go out, could have arranged for social activity during the week so that she would have been ready to stay at home with Patrick on the weekends. At work she could have cultivated women with similar interests. Eating out with them, bowling, playing bridge, getting involved in political matters—whatever her tastes demanded—could have given Donna the social expansion that she denied herself by sitting home waiting for Patrick to show her a good time.

Patrick could have made some adjustments too. He did not need to spend every weekend at home. He could have developed a pattern that permitted him to rest on alternate weekends. That way Donna could have looked forward to two weekends out a month. Their marriage had not moved, though, beyond the dating pattern of their courtship. Each of them expected the other to pretend to be having a good time. If they had explored the choices available to them, they could have avoided the tension that destroyed their mutual affection and turned them into competitors for pleasure instead of lovers.

Although separate working patterns were the external cause of their conflict, *diverse private expectations* also played a part in the failure of their marriage. Patrick had anticipated a marriage like that of his parents—a lovenest arrangement in which the man was the center of attention, pampered and revered by wife and children. Donna, though, earned almost as much as Patrick and expected him to treat her as his social and sexual equal.

During courtship Patrick had deferred to Donna's desires. He had been solicitous of her requests, treating her whims seriously. After the marriage he ceased to care what she wanted to do and became, as far as he was concerned, the head of the household. He saw no contradiction in this change of pattern since it was the one he had observed among most of his middle-class friends. Before the marriage the woman rules; afterward it's the man's turn.

Since their personal expectations differed, Patrick and Donna squabbled over every decision. They developed a *public-private short circuit*. Instead of treating each other like lovers, they treated each other like clients or, at other times, like business competitors. Sometimes they flattered and manipulated each other as if they had something they wanted to sell. Other times they were in fierce competition to see who could spend the most, get by with the most, or win the most friends. They unexpectedly reversed their roles from gentle lover to vicious foe to cause each other pain.

This confusion of professional and private attitudes strained their relationships with others as well as with themselves. In an effort to compensate for the loss of affection at home, Donna began treating other people with excessive kindness. She looked for emotional gratification at the office, and, not surprisingly, the men interpreted her warmth as an indication of her availability.

Patrick's short circuit was more indirect. He compensated for his loss of personal gratification with intensified professional effort. His sales record improved so that he was given several merit increases, which he used to demonstrate his superiority to Donna. She began to see his business success as a challenge to her equality in the marriage—and that is how Patrick wanted her to see it. But his success was not satisfying, and he came to treat sex as though it were a business situation, not an expression of personal concern.

In spite of Patrick's extramarital sexual activity, his sexual tensions increased. And Donna's young teller gave her little satisfaction other than what she derived from cheating on Patrick. In true soap-opera fashion they confessed their infidelities to each other, not so much for the joy of confession as for the joy of hurting each other. In this way their sexuality twisted around to become a source of pain rather than pleasure.

Any of the symptoms that you have seen in Patrick and Donna's marriage should be met head on if you find them in your own. The first step in resolving them is locating the initial causes of the tension. You have the power to control these causes and to turn an unhealthy marriage pattern into a healthy one.

SEXUAL COMPETITION

One of the most frequent causes of sexual tension in two-career marriages is the competitive urge. Joe said, "I let my wife win a card game every night before we go to bed because she's more fun when she wins." As we can see from this statement, Joe enjoys being the superior manipulator who lets his wife win—for his advantage.

If such a marriage works, it's hard to argue with, but sexual game playing can be dangerous. We are trained to view life as competition, from the first report card and little league tournament to the corpse with the showiest casket. Joe's comment illustrates the connection in our culture between public success and private gratification. Joe's wife enjoyed sex more when she was successful than when she was unsuccessful. In this marriage, since Joe let her win, they were both successful in their undertaking.

Just as planned success can enhance sex, so continued failure can lead to frigidity, impotence, or promiscuity. Failure in a competitive society creates a sense of worthlessness or inferiority that can grow into chronic depression. Depression in turn suppresses sexual energy and thus intensifies the general feeling of failure. Such a chronic negative state is often expressed in such destructive behavior as alcoholism, violence, or child abuse.

Success as well as failure can be harmful to sexual expression. Continued success can inflate the ego and lead to unrealistic expectations for sexual gratification. Since the successful person is a winner, he approaches sex with the burden of responsibility on his partner. This overbearing challenge destroys any reciprocal joy and makes the sex act a kind of prostitution.

People whose sex lives are unrewarding can begin a reconstruction effort by ceasing to regard sex as a competitive game. At its best it is an expression of loving concern for the other person. As Thomas More says in his *Utopia*, the highest pleasure is in giving pleasure to others.

Both sex partners, though, must realize that in a world of constant change, every sexual meeting will not be "the greatest." Through a losing streak, we need to remember that every aspect of our lives is reflected in our sexual activity. If we are losing too much, we ought to rearrange our lives so that something goes right. Although we are not in control of every part of our lives, we are capable of isolating that part that is dehumanizing us in some way. That way we can keep our sex life separate from our difficulties.

After all, we are more than the jobs we do. When we see our careers not as the single center of our lives but as only one aspect of a multifaceted existence, we will cease to regard sex as something at which to win. Only then does the winning streak begin.

POWER NEEDS

Whether we are thoroughgoing Freudians or not, we have to admit that sex is a powerful force in our lives. From puberty onward the sex drive is an eight-cylinder engine pulsating in our consciousness. If our public life is going smoothly, we are likely to channel that power into normal, socially acceptable practices that reinforce our sense of an orderly existence. If public pressures mount, we are susceptible to serious sexual dysfunction.

At several universities over the past twenty years, we have watched graduate students try to balance family life with the intense pressure of making a living while writing a dissertation. The resultant pressures sometimes disrupt sexual patterns in strange ways. One student developed an irresistible urge to make obscene telephone calls, another became a voyeur, another made advances to his male students, and several initiated totally unsatisfactory affairs with much younger students.

Most of these practices were temporary and disappeared when the pressure disappeared. And in most of these families the momentary aberration did not destroy the marriage because of the marriage partner's sympathetic understanding. When one member of a couple is under extreme pressure, the other feels tension too. Both must make an effort to work out these tensions, because the preservation of the marriage is more important than any temporary victory over each other. The only way to get through these tense times is to trust in each other and recognize that it is the situation, not the marriage, that is causing the trouble.

Patrick and Donna would have managed their lives more effectively if they had accepted their separate work patterns as something they could either live with or change. Others, given the same situation, adjust their professional lives to each other, either by changing jobs or by accommodating themselves to the existing pattern. We all have the potential for power control; but we have to use it jointly, since mature sex is a joint activity.

SEXUAL CONDITIONING

Because of the richness of our sexual appetite we may sometimes want to be the powerful, forceful member of the union and at other times the dependent, sheltered one. Traditionally, the dependent role has been the woman's and the protective role the man's. Pressures from our culture and from our professional lives tend to restrict us to one of these roles, thus denying us the fullness of sexual expression.

Bennett grew up in a household in which his mother had the children and his father supported the large family by manual labor. From infancy he had been told by his parents that it was sissy to cry. When he accomplished a physical feat, they commended him with some phrase like "That's our little man!" In baseball he was told to "Hit it like a man," and at school he learned to shove and bully his way through.

At his community college, where he was studying engineering, he met Lena. She came from a family in which mother and father interchanged active and passive roles. Her brothers had been given the same warm affection that she had received, and she had seen her father cry several times. From this variety of emotional experience, Lena had developed an expectation of giving and receiving affection.

After their marriage, Bennett's strength, which had initially attracted Lena to him, changed to brutality. He regarded sex as something to be grabbed and devoured. His expectations, developed from what he had known as a boy, made him view Lena as an object designed for his personal gratification. When they were not in bed, she was his property to be protected and displayed.

These contradictory expectations about marriage interfered seriously with their sex lives. Unless Lena was weak and submissive, she did not arouse any erotic response from Bennett. More and more Lena refused to play the subordinate role because she found that his aggressive brutality spoiled her sexual pleasure. "Be gentle," she kept saying, but she was doomed to failure, since twenty years of conditioning had taught him the opposite.

If Bennett and Lena had regarded their marriage to be of higher value than their early training, they could have made progress toward sexual compatibility. Unfortunately, Bennett had no experience in listening to women. Lena was his property, and she should accept her role as his sexual servant. Bennett thought he was making her happy as his father had made his mother happy. Lena was equally unwilling to deny her sexual needs to satisfy Bennett's.

Bennett never saw the possibility of a form of life superior to the one from which he had come. Nothing in his education or his environment had ever hinted at that possibility. Those of us who believe an adequate sexual union is the basis for a full life can make numerous personal adjustments, including rejection of the lifestyle of our parents, to achieve the joy of an equal union, one that permits uninhibited expression of a variety of human emotions.

Besides parental conditioning, our working world also influences our sex life. As always, what happens in our professional lives carries over into our private existence. When Betty and Ralph were married, she was a secretary in an office with seven other women, and he was assistant manager of a department store. He was accustomed to giving orders, and she was accustomed to receiving them. They fell into the submissive woman–dominant man pattern that Lena refused to accept.

Everything went well for the first three years of the marriage. Then Betty was placed in charge of the personnel division of her company. In this job she had to interview applicants of both sexes. Subtle changes began to occur in her relationship with Ralph, sexually and socially. These changes first became obvious at parties. Where, previously, she had permitted him to finish his stories and get the laughs, she now corrected him and interrupted him to make some point of her own. In matters of sex, she became critical and often suggested improvements that would increase her pleasure.

At first Ralph couldn't understand what was happening to Betty. Then he stopped by her office one day while she was interviewing a man several years older than she was and recognized her new professional assurance. Together they discussed her new professional role and how it was affecting the private relationship. What could have been a painful disruption of marital harmony contributed instead to increased personal enjoyment. Instead of sitting quietly after supper listening to Ralph's accounts of his excursions into the world, Betty now had equal time for recounting her professional exploits. They moved from a lovenest relationship to a marriage of state because the job change had given Betty a chance to grow.

The male-female roles we accept in our daily work are powerful forces in conditioning our private lives. Women who are suppressed by men in their professional lives may browbeat their husbands at home. Men who resent having superior women employers sometimes resort to physical violence at home, where they can still hold a woman captive.

Since our sexual needs are conditioned by our family and educational backgrounds as well as by our daily work, the creative force that should arise from sexual expression is often twisted so that it explodes in painful psychological destruction. By declaring our sexual independence from our past and our culture, we can repair the damage done and build toward a strong private unity. Knowledge of possibilities and faith in the basic goodwill of our sex partner are the only essentials for making a fresh start on this central part of public-private existence.

DIVORCE: PERSONAL BANKRUPTCY

The collapse of a marriage almost always involves suffering that is reflected in the professional lives of the two partners who decide to go their separate ways. As always, the professional area is so intimately related to the private one that it may have contributed to the collapse of the marriage. As we have already seen, causes and results are not always easy to establish. What counts is an early awareness of weaknesses that may lead to a marital breakdown.

Whether we marry someone with the same expectations as ours or different ones, whether we have a healthy professional life or a tense one, whether we have a solid sexual basis for our marriage or a confused one, we can still control our choices so that we work toward the central unity that characterizes a solid marriage.

Sometimes, though, either because of our own inability to make a go of it or because of the intractability of our partner, divorce is the only wise choice. We alone can decide when this time comes, but it sometimes helps to talk to friends—several different ones—before we make our decision to end the marriage. Divorce is always painful. And sometimes the scars last a lifetime, on us and others who are touched by it.

Emotional Problems

The emotional problems that accompany the breakdown of a marriage are so numerous and so persistent that we need to be ready for them before they come along. The typical marriage breakdown goes through several stages, as the following example shows.

When Rachel married Randall, she anticipated an exciting career of her own. After several years of marriage, Randall was putting in more and more time getting ahead, and Rachel was stuck in a dead-end job. She had no opportunity for advancement or even for using her present position as a steppingstone to something else. Without knowing it, Rachel had developed a professional competition with Randall and deeply resented his success. She was frequently caustic or sullen. Randall attributed the mood to overwork and suggested that she quit her job. She responded, "My job means as much to me as yours does to you, even though you may not think I'm doing anything important."

In an effort to satisfy her unfulfilled needs, Rachel looked outside her marriage for someone who would appreciate her and make her feel important. She took a lover and made no effort to hide it from Randall.

Randall had endured Rachel's sullenness and sharp tongue, but he was not ready to accept her infidelity. This second stage of the dissolution of their marriage was the most destructive to their emotions. They could endure coldness, wrath, whining, and resentment, but both looked upon infidelity with such horror that it broke them emotionally.

To cover her sense of guilt, Rachel paraded her independence and pretended that her emotional gratification was the center of the universe. She treated her lover and her husband as objects to be manipulated. When the lover moved on to someone else, she could not understand his behavior. She did not realize that he was treating himself to the same kind of emotional independence she had been arguing for.

Randall was in an even more confused state. He still loved Rachel and regarded this stage as a temporary one in a permanent marriage. At the same time, he hated her for what she had done to their marriage. Her infidelity had made all their previous relations suspect to him. He also felt ashamed of being fool enough to endure an unfaithful wife. Social pressure made him believe that divorce was necessary.

The third stage of their emotional breakdown began when Randall started taking divorce seriously. Although Rachel had talked a great deal about independence, she had always assumed that her relationship with Randall was a permanent one. When she knew he was going to leave her, she had second thoughts. The lover meant nothing to her. He was already running around with someone else, and she was extremely jealous and insecure. She hated Randall, but she was afraid of being left alone. What she had was probably better than what she would have after the divorce.

Randall, at this point, cut his emotional ties with Rachel so that he could preserve his own psychic balance. He talked to her when she called him and smiled when they met, but he no longer treated her as a person. This emotional isolationism affected his work and his friendships. He could not express himself openly to others and was frequently out of control emotionally. At work he sometimes became unreasonable and withdrew into his office to sulk.

When the divorce was final, Randall returned to his work with renewed vigor. He gave his daily tasks the emotional energy that he had previously spent on his private troubles. He demanded of himself and others long hours and intense concentration. His superiors admired the way he had come through his emotional difficulties, but some of his friends wondered if the strain didn't show in his new work habits.

Rachel, who had been so eager for emotional and sexual freedom, felt frightened and lonely after the divorce. She had enjoyed tormenting Randall, but now he seemed immune to her wiles. Rachel began calling him and begging for money and attention. She implored him to take her back. She was sure she had done wrong and would not again. Randall, recognizing the old torture pattern, refused to be involved in her life.

These emotional stages are not necessarily part of every marriage collapse, but they are typical enough to be recognizable in many. In this case infidelity was the active cause of the breakup. There are many other possible causes; but generally an unsatisfactory emotional life, for whatever reason, triggers the divorce process.

Professional Problems

The emotional problems that accompany a divorce foster professional ones that aggravate the anguish. Randall and Rachel found that their ability to concentrate was diminished because they were preoccupied with their personal struggle. Everything that happened at work sent their minds back to their private problem. Randall was inclined to see other women through the veil of disillusionment that Rachel had created. Rachel saw the men at work as either female enslavers or sex objects upon whom she could exercise her female charms. Her deep insecurity made her anxious to reassure herself with flirtatious advances that she was still attractive.

This intrusion of the personal into the professional realm, whatever the cause, is an indication that people are losing control. And loss of control means a diminishing of choices. When a tense personal situation like divorce intrudes into your life, you must make an effort to analyze it rationally. You needn't think melodramatically that life is over or that your world view is false. Isolate the cause of the pain and treat it as a temporary, limited condition. By carefully segregating your trouble in a particular compartment, you can go on functioning effectively in other areas of your life.

Legal Problems

In a divorce there are certain unchanging realities. The legal process of separation is one. A lawyer and possibly a marriage counselor will enter into the picture somewhere along the line. These people can relieve some of the pressure, since they treat the divorce with a detached, reassuring professionalism. Both must be chosen wisely, though, or problems can result.

Rachel made the mistake of choosing her divorce lawyer emotionally rather than professionally. She had developed such resentment toward men that she employed a woman lawyer with a long string of feminine liberation cases to her credit. The lawyer incited Rachel to unrealistic expectations of what she should squeeze from her former male jailer. At a crucial time in the divorce, Rachel became aware of her lawyer's extreme position, but it was too late for her to find more judicial legal advice.

Divorce, among other things, is a legal arrangement, just as the marriage was from the beginning. These legal matters need to be free of emotional intrusions, especially in two-career marriages, where both partners have financial investments. You don't need to be vindictive, but neither should you be sacrificial. What is yours by law you should make every effort to retain.

Children are a special problem in divorce because they can't be treated like property. They have emotional lives of their own, and the parental love is strong. Still, for the purpose of the legal settlement, they need to be viewed dispassionately. Under the emotional pressure they may make choices between parents that are unwise. You owe it to your children to choose for them what you honestly believe— independent of your own feelings—is best for them.

How you determine what is best will be difficult. You make this choice the way you make most others, by consultation with people you respect who have been through similar situations or who at least have wide familiarity with the area. The children's teachers, relatives who are closest to them on both sides of the family, and professional counselors can help you make this toughest of choices—deciding about somebody else's life.

Financial Problems

One of the major problems created by a divorce is that of increased financial responsibility. One household is going to become two, and the results of the split will show up in the household budgets. Two can live as cheaply as one only as long as the two live together. Separately, they are independent financial units again.

Problems of this sort can also be handled to a large extent by lawyers. You may have joint charge accounts to convert, loans to renegotiate, and various other financial affairs. Many of these, like changing a name in the telephone book and making adjustments in tax status, are one-time matters. Taking care of them as quickly as possible can help free you of memories of the marriage.

Under the terms of their divorce, Randall signed the insurance policy over to Rachel for as long as she remained single. This arrangement irritated Rachel, because she felt that it should make no difference whether she remarried or not. Nothing in the divorce agreement depended on Randall's remarriage. Thus even financial arrangements can generate emotional explosions.

Interpersonal Relationships

The breakdown of a marriage relationship tends to bring other personal relationships into question as well. Randall was so depressed after his divorce that he was incapable of anything more than self-pity and suspicion. Since Rachel, whom he had known best, has mistreated him, he assumed that all his friends were capable of the same action. He even viewed those who had supported him during his divorce as traitors who had pushed him toward the brink of personal collapse. He ceased to consider other people's feelings and became extremely selfish and demanding.

This reaction is common after a divorce and is an indication of the battering the psyche takes during the separation process. Divorced people can control it to a certain extent by recognizing it for what it is—a reevaluation of their existence. Since marriage was a central part of their being, its dissolution raises questions of some depth. The thoughtless person rushes out and engages in meaningless social activity to try to hide what most people have to face up to—that other people are not always what they seem.

People who have gone through a divorce are dependent more than ever on outside relationships. They should make an effort to find friends with a healthy, positive attitude toward life. Often, in their initial bitterness, divorced people associate with others who make a life out of their resentment. Taking a sincere interest in happy people will reaffirm their belief in the essential goodness of human relationships.

Bitterness sometimes leads to the predatory prowl. People say to themselves, "OK, so I'm going to get what I can before somebody gets me again." A series of exploitations of other people then follows. The divorced person preys upon others, using them either sexually or emotionally for his own pleasure. He can enjoy hurting others as he feels he himself has been hurt.

It is better to say to yourself, "Divorce, like marriage, takes two. Although I've been hurt, some of the fault was mine. I'm going to try now to avoid blame and put the past behind me." That way you can start fresh with other people. The time spent in cultivating deep and lasting relationships with others—of both sexes—will be a wise investment.

You will, of course, find occasion to talk about your former partner, both to old friends and new ones. The sooner you get a formula for referring to that old relationship, the easier it will be for you. "My former husband, Randall," is a good way to start. Then, having identified the relationship, you can talk about Randall as someone who was part of your former life.

You will also have to face up to establishing a new relationship with your former partner. When you meet, as you will, you may as well be civilized. It will do you no good to lie on your former partner's front porch or make threatening phone calls. You must bury the old relationship and develop a cordial distance that will never penetrate the emotional armor of your new life. Gradually you may even enjoy talking to each other about the present.

SECOND MARRIAGE

Second marriages are like second mortgages. They are a high-risk item, but they may yield rich returns. The first time we marry, we usually marry with great hopes and romantic ideals. The second time, we often bring to the commitment serious doubt about our ability to sustain a prolonged relationship.

That doubt may be the residue of bitterness resulting from the divorce or the remains of sorrow over a death. Whether death or divorce ends the first marriage, we are likely to be extremely apprehensive about the success of the second one. We feel that we are on trial to prove that we can make a go of it this time. The person we marry is also on trial—to live up to the previous marriage or to be as different from it as possible.

Awareness of the negative emotions that are likely to accompany second marriages helps us build defenses against their destructive power. These negative feelings stand around us like a wall of old school pictures, haunting us with memories. Only by filling our lives with pictures of the present can we erase these diminishers of our current life.

Fear

Fear is the first, and perhaps most persistent, picture from the past. We are afraid of our ability, afraid of a repeat of our first failure, afraid of life itself. This fear works on us before the marriage, but the marriage cannot allay it. Everything we do, from grocery shopping and budget planning to sex, reminds us of our previous marriage. We have the problem of establishing traditions and patterns that are independent of our past experience. The similarity of the circumstances suggests a constant comparison. But making comparisons will only bring the destructive pattern of the first marriage into the second one.

When Randall remarried, his favorite saying was "Rachel and I used to do it this way." Ann, his new wife, did not understand. She thought he was trying to impose that old pattern on her—as the absolute answer to how things should be done. Naturally, she came to resent the comparisons. Actually, Randall had still not overcome his first marriage and the fear it had created in him of making the same mistakes.

If we recognize this fear for what it is, we can face up to it. A different partner, a different stage of our lives, and so many other changes have made the new marriage very different from the previous one. Past experience can be destructive if it makes us afraid, but it can be extremely useful if we learn from past mistakes. Whether we have had a bad or good first marriage, we need to accept it as part of the past and let it be the foundation of the new one—not its measuring rod. We free ourselves of fear by building faith in our new marriage.

Guilt

Along with the fear that often comes with a second marriage is a persistent sense of guilt. In a first marriage the two partners discover the world with each other, moving out of their innocence into shared experience. In a second marriage the partners come from different worlds, worlds in which they have both made mistakes and experienced guilt. Especially when children are involved, this sense of guilt can be so intense as to threaten the success of the second marriage. Like fear, guilt is a condition we can accept or reject. We have the choice of dwelling continuously on destructive self-condemnation or of moving free from it into a new life.

In some divorces, where ill-will has been generated, the participants try to exploit that sense of guilt. While he was married to Abbie, Herb had an affair with Kate, who became pregnant. When Abbie found out, she took her two teenage boys and left Herb. After the divorce she sent him pictures of the boys and said in the accompanying letters what a loss it was to them that these two innocents had to suffer for Herb's foolishness. If he came to visit them, she said he was a bad influence on them. If he did not come to visit, she wrote that he was neglecting them. Her punishment kept Herb in such a state of guilt that he punished his new wife and child in turn, frequently becoming angry with them or withdrawing.

Herb was guilty, but that condition did not have to spoil his future life. Abbie was guilty too, of vindictiveness. Herb should have recognized Abbie's malice as one of the traits that led to the failure of their marriage. Had Herb been able to accept the reality of Abbie's shortcomings—and his—he might have been able to overcome his guilt.

Self-Righteousness

Persistent faith that marriage can work will help us fight fear and guilt. But this faith has to be in love, not in self-righteousness. Many second marriages fail because people remarry for the wrong reasons. They are determined to prove that they can remarry sooner, richer, or better than the person they divorced.

This competitive spirit, fine in the marketplace, can have unfortunate consequences when it is transferred to the private sphere. Marriage cannot be run like a business, where bullheaded determination is often the only way to beat out that opposition. In marriage we have to have a sincere concern for another person. If we marry to prove ourselves right, we are exploiting the person we marry.

Self-righteousness is a standard handicap in second marriages. Naturally, divorce may leave some bitterness, but we must control it before we start again. We have to ask ourselves, "Am I going with this person because of my first marriage?" If the answer is yes, we must slow down and get control over these destructive emotions.

Second marriages begun in fear, guilt, or self-righteous determination can survive, but it is much better to recognize these negative qualities in our new relationship and overcome them as soon as possible. Second marriages have enough challenges of their own.

As we begin a second marriage, we must remind ourselves that we are not the same person we were the first time we married. Some people think they can reclaim their youth by marrying a younger person the second time. They may have had a state marriage the first time, then decide at forty-five that they would prefer a lovenest relationship. Either type can work—but only if both partners accept it.

Second marriages for people with two careers are often complicated by the fact that both participants are well-established professionally. Being established in a professional position makes adjustments at the private level easier. When people are just beginning a career at the same time they are beginning a marriage, the tensions are doubled. In a second marriage, career strains should have given way to career satisfactions.

Sometimes, though, professional success brings with it a certain inflexibility that makes personal readjustment difficult. After the death of his first wife, Ivan told his friends that he would not think of marrying again. Two years later, at a convention, he met a public relations specialist and rapidly fell in love with her. He was a corporation vice president, fifteen years older than she; but they agreed after the first few dates that age was not a significant matter. As it happened, not age but professional differences were the handicap in the marriage.

It was Amy's second marriage too. She had been married for a short time when she was quite young and since that time had pursued her interest in her career. To her it was as important as Ivan's. From the beginning, he expected her to defer to him in career matters, and she soon found that he didn't respect her work. As a result, she became jealous and resentful of his. His fatherly condescension was a major irritant in their marriage.

Happiness is a delicate and temporary condition. We can foster it by rejecting the negative attitudes that stifle it, or we can wallow in self-pity over the past. We owe it to our new marriage to put the old one behind us and try to cultivate a sensitivity to our second partner's needs. With faith in our ability to adjust, we can make our new marriage a happy one.

The Joneses Talk About Sex, Divorce, and Second Marriage

Ruth: I think the point we've been trying to make in this chapter is that marriages are more likely to last if we don't assume that the role we play at work is the same one we're going to play at home.

Bill: You mean we should protect our marriage by keeping it in a separate compartment from our work?

Ruth: Not exactly a separate compartment, but we should realize that just because someone is boss at work he isn't necessarily boss at home.

Bill: That may be desirable, but I think we both know plenty of people whose professional lives determine their expectations at home. A department head who is in the habit of getting respectful silence when he talks is likely to be the dominant authoritarian at home too.

Ruth: If he is, he's confusing the role at work with his real identity. He assumes that because he has been granted some power to control he is powerful himself. When he has to relinquish that power, either through retirement or transfer, he will feel he's lost his identity. That is, he will unless he has maintained a healthy awareness of himself through other contacts—at home and in nonprofessional social situations.

Bill: You're right. People would be much better off if they cultivated the necessary professionalism at work but concentrated on a variety of private relationships outside their work.

Ruth: Talking about relationships, do you think we've made second marriage sound like an impossible undertaking?

Bill: We've been quite realistic in our observations, but I hope we've made the point that love is always possible. People have to free themselves of the painful memories of previous relationships, though, and look with honest expectation at present possibilities.

Ruth: Well, we've talked about everything in this chapter quite openly. We may have made sex seem forbidding too.

Bill: Well, we've tried to point out that compartmentalization is not a realistic possibility in any of the areas where career and marriage overlap. Even though it may be desirable to have different personalities at home and at work, they are interrelated parts of one life.

Ruth: I don't think you have different personalities at home and at work. You don't want to be "more yourself" at one place than the other. If you did, you'd feel one was a less true expression of yourself.

Bill: That's right. Sex can be the most private expression of self while professional achievement is the most public expression, but I still maintain that it's all the expression of only one identity—one personality.

Ruth: I think the distinction needs to be kept clear. We are never more or less ourselves, or if we are we're not fooling anybody but ourselves. That may be the reason for so much unhappiness and divorce—everybody else sees what we refuse to admit to ourselves.

Bill: I hope this chapter has brought enough light so that we can all see more clearly.

5

Children and Working Parents

CHILDREN are a special problem for two-career parents because our society is still largely constructed on the assumption that the mother will stay home to care for the children. At a time when it takes two incomes to maintain a family, children may seem more a burden than a blessing. Although our culture has not arranged as well for substitute parents as some other cultures have, arrangements can be made so that two-career families will be able to enjoy their children.

Having children or not having them is a matter that each two-career couple must decide for itself. It is very easy to permit societal pressures to force the choice one way or the other. Those with children will sometimes try to make the childless couple see how much they're missing, but those without children can also make the harried parent envious.

To have children to satisfy your relatives or to keep up with your peers is hardly a valid reason for doubling or even tripling the size of your family. You shouldn't have a child until you both want one for its own sake. And you should be willing to accept the drastic change in life that is bound to come with it. The relatives who are urging you to become parents won't have to get up for night feedings. And those proud parents who brag about their baby aren't telling you how many diapers they have to change. Parents sometimes praise parenthood for the same reason married people praise marriage—to convince themselves they did the right thing.

In parenthood, as in other areas of marriage and career, the right choices for others are not necessarily the right ones for you. The time to have children is when you have established yourselves professionally so that you will be able to afford them and enjoy them.

FOR OR WITH THE CHILDREN?

One of the first choices that arises after you decide to have children is whether you believe you are working *for* your children or *with* them. This choice will determine your parental relationship for the rest of your lives. Al and Claudia fell into the habit of thinking of their first child as their boss. "She's so demanding about feeding time," Claudia used to say about her daughter. Al told his friends that baby Angela was such a lady she couldn't stand dirty diapers for a minute.

This initial subservient pattern continued as Angela grew up. Out of their sincere devotion to their daughter, Al and Claudia made a game of serving her. When Angela went off to nursery school, Al prepared a breakfast of her choice while Claudia consulted her about what she wanted to wear that day. Al and Claudia became competitors for approval from their boss, wooing her with overtime labor and reminding her of their special contributions to her happiness.

Al and Claudia were most anxious to please when they had not done well at work. Angela became the after-hours boss whose appreciation could be gained when the real boss was grouchy or inaccessible. This transfer from public to private life was not apparent to Al and Claudia, who were simply satisfying a need for approbation that was not being met through their work.

Such a transfer, however, can be quite dangerous. When Angela became boss, she was placed in a position for which she had no experience. Soon she began to think that the world was designed to serve her, since at first everyone she saw was eager to please her. As a result of this false start, she had difficulty making social adjustments at nursery school. This difficulty drove Al and Claudia to even more frenzied efforts to please their boss at home. Thus they widened the gap for Angela between the unrealistic home situation and the painfully realistic public one.

The boss-employee relationship does not permit the growth of natural affection. We try to please our boss, but we sometimes feel resentful when he doesn't respond with the gratitude we expect. Such a situation soon developed for Angela. She gladly accepted the services provided her, but her parents demanded from her more and more visible assurance that they were pleasing her. "Tell me that you love me," they pleaded. "Give Daddy a kiss for bringing you the water." Such expressions became the standard demand that Angela's employees made on her gratitude. Before long, Angela's responses to interpersonal relationships became superficial and hollow; she was incapable of expressing genuine warmth in human contacts. A real emotion would have shattered the fragile illusion of her home life.

A healthy parent-child relationship requires more flexibility than Al and Claudia gave it. Certainly, in the first years of a child's life, the child needs its parents' attention. Angela could not have fed herself her bottle or changed her own diapers. But the parental attitude toward these required duties determines from the beginning how successful the parent-child collaboration will be.

Parents are not an infant's employee; they are co-workers in the business of growing up. You are cooperating with your child in a process that will gradually lead to his physical and emotional independence. Together you move through a series of shifting patterns necessary for successful living in the private sphere. You change the baby's diapers not because he demands that they be changed but because his cries let you know that they need changing. You thus work *with* him toward a healthy future. The same is true of infant feeding. The baby is not demanding that you run to take care of his needs; he is giving you the only indication he knows—a cry—that his system needs refueling.

Although it is not easy, it is possible to shift from the unhealthy boss pattern to the more rewarding co worker system. By the time Angela was thirteen, her position as her parents' boss had made her unbearable. She would not listen to their advice but was too inexperienced to make decisions of her own. She had antagonized every authority figure in her world and had grown more and more wretched because of her failure to establish pleasant relationships. She lashed out frequently at her parents, who shrank, like the unsatisfactory employees they were, into the nearest corner to avoid the wrath of their superior.

In desperation, after one of Angela's temper tantrums, Al and Claudia went to a child psychiatrist. He pointed out the flaw in the relationship, the one we have observed from the beginning. The psychiatrist pointed out that Angela was searching for an authority figure upon whom she could rely for guidance. The natural place for a child to seek such aid is at home. When Angela did not find it there, she rebelled against people who occupied positions similar to those of her parents. She was therefore incapable of accepting the guidance of her teachers or other adults and listened instead to the poor advice of other adolescents.

It was not easy for Al and Claudia to overcome their early errors of seeing the child as boss instead of co-worker, but the problem had become so serious that they were willing to make the effort. For the first time, they imposed definite rules for family living. They enforced the rules by withholding the privileges that Angela had previously assumed were her inalienable rights. When she was denied her allowance, a trip to visit relatives, and other treats she began to see that living in a family is a cooperative arrangement rather than an autocratic one.

By the time she finished high school Angela was a great deal more tractable. She had learned from her parents that the rewards of social adjustment are peaceful evenings of laughter around the dinner table and helpful advice from anyone in the family who happens to understand the crisis best. Beyond the family, these changes made Angela more sympathetic and understanding and far less demanding. She began to develop friendships in which she was able to give and receive affection. The result was an improvement for the whole family.

WORKING-FAMILY GUILT

The story of Angela and her parents is a common one among working couples, who sometimes feel guilty that they are not giving their children as much attention as they should. This misunderstanding about the nature of parenthood often leads to overcompensation.

As the standard family pattern changes, it is quite possible to make arrangements for children so that they do not have to be under the constant supervision of a parent. Queen Elizabeth II of England, for example, regularly allotted one hour a day to her children. She saw them occasionally at other times, but maternal duties were assigned to substitute parents.

As long as children are reasonably supervised, parents should feel free to pursue their careers without guilt. You may feel some disappointment, of course, at not being able to spend more time with your children, but such a longing can enrich the relationship by making you cherish the time you have. You may also want to spend more time with the person you're married to, or with your mother, or at the movies, or in the tub. But life is limited by time, and you have to make wise choices about how to use what time you have.

If you truly enjoy the time with your children, and they enjoy it too, you are contributing positively to their development—no matter how short that time is. If someone else feeds them lunch and keeps them from running in the street, you need not feel guilty. You are paying for that substitute service with money earned from your profession. You should view these choices as reasonable alternatives to a lovenest marriage.

Whatever your decision, you should accept it as a matter of personal choice and not let guilt or societal pressure influence you. Just as wise couples make their own choice about when to have children, so they make their own choice about what to do with them after they have them. Because your parents did it a certain way is no reason to follow suit. Your family represents a new generation. Together you and your partner must decide what is right for you and, having made that decision, live happily with it.

WORKING-FAMILY AMBIGUITY

Although two-career families need not adopt a Victorian concept of mother-father division of responsibility, some regular pattern does need to be visible to children. Otherwise, children can become confused about parental identities. Linguists have found that a young child will learn two languages easily if one parent always speaks one language to him and the other speaks a different one—all the time. If he does not always hear each parent in a single language, linguistic confusion results so that the child cannot distinguish one language from the other.

The same holds true for mother-father roles in the family. Children are learning constantly about order in the universe, and they are not instantly ready for the complexity of modern living. They like to see the father doing the same things around the house week after week and the mother doing different things. If the two parents perform without differentiation in the child's observation, he has trouble distinguishing one from the other.

The ambiguity is not necessarily harmful, but we need to be aware of it. Child and parent alike need some sense of order in family activities. This order can be achieved if we consciously assume regular family duties. When two parents come home from work to spend a limited amount of time with their children, they can save energy by taking assignments that come naturally to each of them. Doing these assignments regularly helps the child differentiate between parents.

Still, some substitution can be valuable. If the father reads regularly to the child at bedtime, the mother should occasionally fill in. This way the child learns order without rigidity. Children who grow up in flexible households do not narrowly classify certain tasks as men's or women's. These children learn that jobs are taken according to interest and ability. As they grow older, they then assume their roles in the family unit for the same good reason—something needs to be done, and they don't mind doing it.

ANALOGY LIVING

As we saw earlier, Al and Claudia treated their daughter Angela as though she were their boss and they were assigned to please her. Instinctively, when we enter a new stage of life, we apply to it an approach that seems appropriate from earlier experiences. The result is frequently a transfer between our private lives and our public ones. Such a transfer could be called "analogy living" because it builds on similarities.

Analogy living may be destructive or constructive, depending on how valid the transfer is. In Angela's case, an inappropriate analogy of child as boss put a strain on Angela and her parents. On the other hand, by regarding her as a co-worker, Al and Claudia were able to correct some of the errors they made with their first analogy.

In relationships with children, false and valid analogies are constantly suggesting themselves, since patterns of living make action easier and more efficient. The one sure way to judge analogies is by their results—for ourselves and others. The rest of this chapter is devoted to the investigation of some of the most common child-parent analogies. From these examples you can decide which ones might be useful for your own family at various stages of development.

CHILD AS RAW MATERIAL

When a child is very small, parents tend to treat him as raw material to be molded into a finished product. The child is growing so rapidly that he seems like a mass of clay spinning on a potter's wheel.

During infancy, this manufacturing analogy works quite well. The doctor's prescriptions for the child's care are instructions to be followed for processing the raw material. You are busy with the diet that makes him grow, the sleep that keeps him healthy, and the words that make him capable of communication. He knows no food you do not give him and no words that are not imitations of your own.

After two or three years, though, you are not the only craftsmen shaping the raw material. In nursery school he begins to receive other, sometimes contradictory, messages. You have always felt it best to give him no snack in the afternoon. Now you hear that he is getting milk and cookies in school at three-thirty. You have always watched your language around the child. Now he comes home with some shocking expletives he's learned at nursery school.

At that point you have to accept the limitations of the raw material analogy. You are no longer a solitary craftsman creating a beautiful object. You are but one member of an assembly-line crew working on something that you will never be able to shape to your complete satisfaction. The sooner you accept this shift, the happier you and the child will be.

Bert and Trish dreamed of having their first son grow up to be a physician. Bert had never been able to afford medical school, but he worked and saved for his son's education. Long before their son reached college, though, it should have been obvious to Bert and Trish that Brent was not interested in a professional career—unless it was in baseball. When Brent was six, his father gave him a doctor set for Christmas, but the only part Brent liked was the stethoscope. He made a slingshot out of it and broke a window with it. Two years later he traded his doctor set for a baseball glove.

These early indications that their raw material had a will of its own did not deter Trish and Bert from trying to shape Brent into the product they had anticipated from his birth. In spite of his bad math record in high school, Brent was shoved into a college that specialized in premedical education—where he joined a fraternity and a softball team.

Although Bert had spent a lot of time dreaming about his son the doctor, he had spent even more time watching sports on TV and talking about ball scores with his friends. From early childhood, Brent had heard a lot more about the World Series than about health service possibilities. In other words, Bert was shaping his raw material far more effectively by his actions than by his unrealistic dreams.

When Brent flunked out of his prestigious college and tried out for a ball club, his mother and father felt that their product had been spoiled. In their failure to understand the assembly-line process rather than the single craftsman approach, they branded their son an ungrateful failure.

Brent didn't feel like a failure at all. He had always known what he wanted to do, but near the top of his priority list was the desire to please his parents. These contradictory urges made Brent tense and difficult to live with. Only after he gave up trying to fit into the mold set by his parents did he become the happy, relaxed person that his parents had wanted him to be all along.

Although the raw material analogy is useful for some aspects of a child's development, it is limited. The child is not simply a piece of material to be cut to a preconceived form. As we shall see later, the child has a will of his own that shapes his character, just as cloth has a nap and wood a grain. When we turn the nap the wrong way or cut against the grain, we are in for some disappointments in the finished product.

CHILD AS TOOL

Sometimes, instead of seeing their children as material to mold into shape, parents see them as tools, instruments to aid them in their efforts to achieve something in life. In our professional careers we can't get a job done without the right equipment. Whether it is a computer, a Xerox machine, or a typewriter, certain jobs require certain equipment. It is easy for parents to begin equating their children with a typewriter or a calculator.

The tendency may begin even before the children are born. Ted says to Fay, "We'll never get my mother off our backs till we have a baby. She's got to be a grandmother." Fay is happy in her job and satisfied with her life with Ted. She wants to please Ted, even though she doesn't care about his mother. She delays for a while, but gradually she becomes convinced that the family relationship will be improved if she gets pregnant. Thus begins the first step in using children as tools to get a job done. Ted's mother is happy—for the moment.

The danger of using children this way is that it may lead us to regard them as a means to an end rather than something of value in themselves. Children suffer from such a depersonalized attitude. They can cease to function effectively unless they are reassured frequently that they are more important for what they are than for what they can do. If we give them the impression that we love them because they are quiet in company or because they perform well on the potty chair, they respond to us mechanically, satisfying our functional demands but growing remote and alienated.

Some people unconsciously use their children as extensions of their own desire to achieve. When we drive our child to win in little league ball or insist on good grades in school, we should be sure that we are urging these accomplishments for the sake of the child and not to gratify our own unfulfilled desires. We can force our children into behavior patterns that we think are right for them simply because we want the sense of success that comes from getting achievement points in our family.

The kind of tool parents make out of their children is often related to their personal strivings. Parents who are anxious to get ahead socially are probably educating their children to achieve in social relationships. One family spent far more money than they could afford sending their children to a prestigious summer camp where two socially prominent families from town regularly sent their children. The mother derived great pleasure from telling her friends that her children were driving home with these social leaders and used the relationship to advance her stock with the country club set.

Such behavior is usually more obvious to the children than the social climbers realize. In this family the children knew why they were going to camp and resented their parents' manipulation, misbehaving and rebelling so that the project backfired.

Other parents use their children to excuse their own behavior. A father says, "I wouldn't do this except for my children." A mother says, "The only reason I work as hard as I do is for my children." Using children as an excuse results in antagonism between parent and child. When a nail goes in crooked, a carpenter will often fling his hammer to the ground in disgust. That's how some parents react when they find that their children are not doing the job for them that they want done—making them feel useful and successful. Children who fail their parents in this way are often abused, neglected, or otherwise mistreated.

Parents who view the child as a tool forget that he is a responsive individual with a mind of his own. They are using the child like a plane or a sander to smooth the way for themselves, not for him. Children know this intuitively and often refuse to perform, so that the effort usually roughens rather than smooths the family relationship.

CHILD AS CUSTOMER

We have already talked about regarding children as though they were bosses, but we sometimes treat them as customers. This analogy produces a similar subservient relationship. The main difference is that with a customer we are selling something, a product or our services. With a boss all we are trying to do is please so that we can obtain a more generous reward for services rendered.

Marsha and David were childless for seven years before they had their son Malcolm. They loved him more than anything else in the world. Their professional lives had been successful, and they were well-off financially. Although they still worked hard, they had the leisure to enjoy Malcolm, who the doctors said would be their only child.

At first they worked together to shower him with their products—love, affection, favors, and advertisements of their wares. "Won't it be fun when we go to the zoo Saturday?" they would say, working on their customer as early as Monday or Tuesday. By Saturday they had overadvertised their product so much that the zoo was bound to be a disappointment. Before he went to nursery school, Malcolm was jaded. Marsha and David had flooded their customer with so many products that he was tired of them all.

Then the competition began. Marsha and David ceased to run the same business and became competing salesmen. "I think he loves you more than he loves me," Marsha would say in a worried tone. Then she would try some new advertising campaign to win Malcolm back.

The friendly parental competition soon became cutthroat. By the time Malcolm went to school, each parent was selling him love with high-pressure sales techniques. If David took him to a ballgame on Saturday, Marsha had a special pie ready for his supper when they got home. It was not long before each one began knocking the competition. Marsha's favorite put-down was "Oh, that's the way your father is." And David's attention-getting mechanism was "Women just don't understand."

Torn between the two competitors for his love, Malcolm learned that he could get a bargain price by negotiating for what he wanted. He could manipulate his parents by playing their services against each other. But the surplus of service did not make Malcolm happy. He was like a consumer whose icebox is stuffed with delicacies he hasn't eaten but who is still urged to buy more by the frantic salesmen working the market. Malcolm needed to know the joy of scarcity.

Fortunately, he survived this treatment as customer and went off to college, where he was relieved to find that people were not out to sell him anything. They offered only friendship and human civility. The change from the high-pressure salesmanship of his youth was refreshing. When he came home the first Christmas, he said, "Stop fighting over me. I love you both and wish you'd leave me alone."

David and Marsha reacted as if their major market had just been closed down. But Malcolm treated them with careful reserve and learned to create the kind of customer-salesman relationship he could live with. David and Marsha had been treating him as customer too long to change, but Malcolm changed once he got out from under their influence.

At times, all of us treat our children as if they were customers. After all, children are the consumers of our time and effort. The danger lies in adopting this attitude too much of the time and not recognizing its limitations. If children are indeed our customers, they are fortunate to have our services. We have a limited clientele, and it is as much their privilege to be served as it is ours to serve them. If we can maintain that attitude of reciprocity, we will have satisfied customers who appeciate our product—parenthood.

CHILD AS SUBSTITUTE SELF

Sometimes in management we are inclined to generalize about what others want by determining what we would do in a similar situation. We may anticipate a market demand, for example, by saying, "If I were buying, I'd certainly like to have one of these." Such a narrow survey technique is almost invariably disappointing. We are generalizing from only one example. We are not the market, and we cannot see clearly beyond our own hopes for success with our product. It is better to spend time taking representative samples to make sure our production efforts are going to pay off.

When we treat our children as though they were our substitute selves and try to decide for them, the narrow view leads to difficulties. We are not their age, nor are they ours, so the differences make substitute self a false analogy.

Bea and Dan used the substitute-self theory with their daughter Tammy. "You have to have rest now," Bea used to tell Tammy when Tammy was three. "If I'd played as long as you, I'd be exhausted. Come in now and lie down." The fact that Tammy was carrying around thirty pounds and Bea a hundred and thirty did not enter into Bea's consideration. She assumed Tammy was ready for a rest because she would have been.

This assumption of identical response is not usually harmful when children are small. When they reach adolescence, though, they resent the false attributions. When Tammy was twelve, she was ashamed of the dark fuzz on her legs. Several of her friends suggested that she follow their example and start shaving. "Don't be silly," her mother said. "I didn't start shaving till I was fourteen. You're much too young for that."

Bea was blonde, but Tammy was dark like her father. Bea's only yardstick, however, was herself. She assumed that Tammy was trying to grow up too soon. This false analogy led to embarrassment and resentment for Tammy, who finally rebelled and bought her own razor. When Bea found out, she flew into a rage. "I never disobeyed my parents the way you disobey us," she screamed. And what should have been a natural maturation process became a major family conflict into which even the hesitant Dan was drawn.

By the time Dan got involved, Bea had muddled the situation so that neither she nor Tammy could remember the origin of the quarrel; all they knew was their immediate anger. Tammy's standard response was "You don't understand that things are different now, Mom." But her mother refused to listen to that essentially sound argument.

Things are always different, and each situation has to be considered in terms of the needs of the people involved. Bea would have been wrong simply to agree to everything Tammy demanded, but she should not have set up a false standard of judgment and then closed her mind to Tammy's needs.

When our children arrive at the stage of sexual awareness, we grow especially apprehensive, hoping they will not fall prey to errors we have made in that area—or errors we have seen others make. Consequently, we sometimes put galling restrictions on our children when sympathetic understanding is most needed. Instead of a blanket statement such as "I was never permitted to act like that," we could take the time to ask, "Why do you want to do this?" Thus we might find out about the changing modes of behavior that are now challenging our children.

We keep our children's confidence best when we are able to point out dangers they will have to face. They will be more likely to listen if we assure them that we know they want to do the right thing. As they move through school, unless they are sure we know the right thing, they will attach more significance to the values of their friends than to those of their family. When that happens, we cannot fall back on the substitute-self idea; we must try to see the world from their point of view. Otherwise, we are bound to lose their confidence.

In addition to making decisions on the assumption that our children are like we are, we may sometimes misuse them by trying to make them what we wanted to be—another form of self-substitution. Perhaps the quickest way to alienate a child is to force him into the life we wanted to live—and demand his gratitude in the bargain. Bea's attitude toward Tammy became that way, partly because from the beginning she had established the idea of Tammy as her substitute self. "I don't want Tammy to have to do without things the way I did," Bea said. "I'm going to work hard to see that she gets everything I never had."

And then the misunderstandings grew. Tammy had to take voice lessons, which she hated, and ballet, which she hated, because her mother had always wanted to be able to sing and dance. Tammy's interests were inclined toward practical business matters. By the time she was fourteen she had her own paper route after school and regarded having to get substitutes while she went to ballet and voice as nothing but an expensive inconvenience.

Bea felt Tammy should be grateful for her cultural opportunities. She certainly would have been. It was not easy for her to see that she and Dan had educated Tammy to care more for the money than for the lessons money could buy. Tammy's eagerness to take the paper route and to accumulate a bank account were the outgrowth of a pattern she had seen in her family as long as she could remember. Her mother was trying to shape Tammy into something else. We have to accept the fact that our children are likely to become not what we *want* them to be but what they see in us. If we are accumulating money for its own sake, as Bea and Dan were, we should not be surprised if our children place the same value on accumulating money.

We are so much more forceful than our children that we can usually make them believe they want what we always wanted. Alma had always wanted to be a New York model. As a young woman, she had modeled in her hometown, but she had never been able to get the money together to go to New York. Her daughter Bette grew up listening to stories about the good pay and the thrills of modeling. She also grew up as an extremely devout member of her father's church, where he was a faithful minister.

The two patterns of life began to conflict when she was in college. Bette became convinced that she should leave her major in religion and try modeling while she was still young enough to make it big. With help from friends, she got to New York, to discover that she had to change in front of male photographers. She was expected to model underwear of varying degrees of transparency, and she was constantly besieged by the men with whom she worked. Although she had some of the requirements for success as a model, her religious orientation made it impossible for her to work easily in the fleshly world of the city.

Alma was wise enough to recognize these conflicts and surrender in time to permit Bette to come home. Unfortunately, she had imposed her desire so strongly on her daughter that Bette became a self-substitute in the most frightening sense of the term—a child so completely another self that she internalizes her parent's desires as her own. Bette spent years recovering from a sense of failure that she would not have had to face if she had been allowed to shape her own desires rather than living out those of her mother.

We see our children in terms of our own experiences at their age, but we do not always see their tremendous dependence on us for emotional security. The world is a threatening place at the age of ten or fourteen. Our children need, as we needed, the firm backing of their family against the threat of the outside world. If we see our children as ourselves, then we should see that being alienated from our parents is the darkest and most desperate experience of our lives.

Seeing our children's needs in terms of our own experience is positive and rewarding. Trying to impose on them the half-remembered dreams and ambitions of our youth is a dangerous and probably impossible task. It is much better to enjoy our children as they are—growing creatures separate from ourselves but a part of the world we inhabit.

PARENTS AS BANKERS

One of the obvious relationships with our children is the financial one. We are the holders of the funds they need to engage in the business of growing up. Like bankers, we have to finance projects, determine good risks, and give financial advice.

First of all, the financing. Different kinds of parents have produced well-adjusted children with quite different attitudes toward the extent of their financial responsibility. Some parents feel they should give their children unlimited credit. They provide open accounts with a perpetual minimum balance. Some of these children turn out to be spendthrifts; others develop a rational appreciation for things money can do because they have had a lot of experience with it.

For those who want to give their children everything, the amount given is not as significant as the way in which it is given. If children are brought up to understand that possessions are obtained through the wise handling of money, they can receive a great deal without becoming spoiled by the capitalist process. If they are never educated in the way money works, they will become prodigal in their habits and irresponsible financially. One of the banker's jobs is to provide periodic statements so that his account holders know what their balance is.

The time to start these statements varies with the family. One family we know began informing the children when they were quite small that they were taken care of only until they finished college. After that, their accounts in the family bank were closed. Another family criticized this approach and said that it could make the children insecure. They felt that children should be carried on account as long as they needed the support.

Both families have seen their children develop into responsible, independent operators. Whether we give them all or a limited checking account, we need to provide them with a systematic statement on which they can rely. And it should be businesslike. Financial support should not be an emotional issue. We should decide what we can afford to give our children and then make it clear to them that this is the way the account works.

Unlike the family that can give their children unlimited checking privileges, most of us are on limited funds. Even though we may regret not being able to be more generous with our children, we can teach them to be satisfied with a small amount if they see that we are distributing money equitably. One member of the family must not be receiving luxuries while the others are surviving on handouts. A family banking unit must be based on equal shares, or at least justifiable differences. Irrational and emotional discrepancies cause resentment and bad banking.

Besides providing checking privileges to our children, we have to determine risk. Banking is more than handing out money; it is deciding what is likely to pay reasonable dividends and what is likely to fail. With our children we have to start early making these judgments about our investments. The more conscious we are of the choices and their consequences, the better bankers we're going to be with our children.

A few investments are generally accepted as essential for children. We have to expect medical bills, dental bills, school expenses, and a clothing allowance. Within these acceptable areas we have to make choices. The clothing that is simply wearing apparel in the third grade becomes a prestige item later on. When this change occurs, we have to realize that no amount of money spent on clothes is going to buy the child total security.

We know one girl who left forty T-shirts in her drawer after she had selected those she wanted to take with her to camp. In this case the family banker was lax in his supervision of the clothing account. To determine what is good and bad for our children, we have to know them. If they tend to substitute purchases for more lasting pleasures, it is our duty to guide them away from these bad habits. And we can recognize the danger signals only if we are in close communication with them.

We should never let money become a substitute for personality development. A poor banker sometimes gets the impression that he need only give his children sufficient funds to settle their problems. "Be quiet and I'll buy you a piece of candy," a mother says to her three-year-old as they shop in the supermarket. "Don't argue with me, and I'll buy you a new stereo for Christmas," a busy father tells his son to close an argument.

Only by giving our children our time as well as our money are we going to get to know them. We don't have to be alike to love each other. One of the happiest father-son combinations we know is a conservative investor named Gus whose liberal son Ace has a Ph.D. in urban sociology. These two have developed a close relationship because from the beginning Ace recognized his father's loving attention. They shared years of fishing together, trips to ballgames, and visits to the farm to take care of the horses. These activities were filled with such happy conversations on noncontroversial subjects that controversy took its rightful place outside the relationship.

While Ace was growing up, Gus and he were sympathetic friends. Advice flowed freely both ways.

When Ace took his first cigarette, Gus knew about it and had a talk with him. "Your grandfather died of a heart attack at fifty-five," Gus said, "and your heart is made of the same kind of material his was. I know now that fifty-five seems a long way off, but I'm only five years from that. Don't you want me to live longer than five more years? You owe it to your own children to think again about smoking."

"But all my friends think I'm a sissy if I don't smoke," Ace said.

"I know." Gus was not contemptuous of this legitimate teenage concern. "The only thing to do is to show them in other ways that you aren't one. Let's take them out to the farm and let them see you ride."

The advice was solid and successful because it was not superficially handed out. Gus considered the total social situation and responded out of sympathetic concern. He knew we have to show children love and understanding in a nonjudgmental way if we are to catch errors early on.

And we can expect rebellion at several places along the line. Growing up is not easy. Peer pressure, especially when it contradicts parental pressure, can be overwhelming. On those occasions we must be patient and give our children the benefit of the doubt. We should credit them with good intentions and continue to support them, even when they are resentful or difficult. If our good advice is not followed, we can exert financial pressure. The temporary suspension of the child's allowance usually reduces the risk factor. We are always in a superior bargaining position. As bankers we have the last word.

PARENTS AS CONSULTANTS

The banker analogy leads to the one that works best for all ages—that of consultant. We may sometimes have to use financial pressure to achieve our purpose, as bankers do; we may occasionally even profit from treating our children as raw material, customers, or self-substitutes. But for everyday relations the best attitude is that of consultant. We are more experienced in living than the young creatures who are under our care. We can therefore offer them good advice that comes out of that experience.

But they have to ask for it. And the only way they are going to request us to serve as consultants is if we demonstrate honestly that we have information from which they can benefit. No one wants a consultant who can't manage his own business, and children can see when their parents have botched their own lives. One of our friends' children once remarked, "Negative examples are all my parents' marriage has ever given me."

When a specialist goes to a company as a consultant, he is asked there because of his experience; but his experience is useless unless he takes the time to understand current conditions in the particular business. He has to pay a site visit, or at least look at the appropriate records, before he can apply his previous experience to the present need. As parents, we are in the same position. Our advanced knowledge of life does us no good unless we take the time to study the situation our children now face and speak to that need—not to one that ceased to exist years ago.

The consultant analogy works because we are ahead of our children in living and have been through situations similar to their own. Still, we must always be willing to consider differences as the child grows up. What was right for us may not be appropriate under changed conditions. One woman we know still dresses her daughter the way Shirley Temple dressed at the age of three, with ribbons in her hair and short, dotted-swiss dresses. The fact that children's styles have changed in forty years has made little impression on this woman, who is stuck with what was right for her and her generation.

In the elementary school years, we have to be extremely sensitive consultants in matters of dress and social behavior. We must talk with other parents who are also trying to see the distinction between what is desirable and what is practiced. Children are uncertain and need guidance, but they are not separated from the herd with which they are running. We may have to settle for occasional success and give in on less significant matters. If we issue close-minded, arbitrary edicts, our children are likely to reject any later suggestions we make. To retain our position as consultants, we must continue to offer our children sound guidance without giving more advice than the situation demands.

Harold loved his job as parental consultant. Every night at supper he asked his son how the day went. No matter what the child said, Harold responded with sanctimonious sermons on the way the situation should have been handled. Teachers, friends, enemies, girlfriends—Harold had something to say on everything. Before Harold's son finished grade school, he had quietly fired his father as consultant. He endured the chatter because it was easier than contradicting a man who was so busy talking that he never listened to his son's needs. As it was, Harold's son turned to the advice of far less qualified consultants—friends his own age.

Above all, consultants must be honest with their clients. They cannot pretend to be infallible. When both parents are working, time and energy are seriously limited. As we've already pointed out, our society is not yet completely geared to two-career marriages. We can make them work, though, by letting our children realize from a very early age that we are people as well as parents—that we have needs and problems just as they do. When we share our limitations with our children, they will come to respect us as consultants and grow up enriched by our two careers rather than deprived by them.

The Joneses Talk About Children

Bill: One of the best mothers I know said she would have given her daughter away when she was a senior in high school. Do you think any parents get through bringing up children without some bad moments?

Ruth: No mother whose child is out in a car can hear an ambulance siren without a catch at her heart. If that's what you mean by "bad moments," we all have them.

Bill: That's not exactly what I mean. I remember your mother saying you never gave her a moment's worry. Do you think she meant it?

Ruth: I know she worried about me. I heard her tell the doctor she was panicky when her children were sick, but whether she worried if I'd turn out all right or not, I don't know. She was so optimistic that I think she always looked for the best. Maybe that's what she meant about my never having given her a moment's worry.

Bill: There are things we can't control, like accidents and sickness, but we correct what we can. The parents who are least in control of their children have the most to worry about.

Ruth: Many parents engage in useless worry. Two friends came to me, extremely worried that their children would be involved in drugs. The objects of their worry ranged in age from six months to six years. Such unrealistic dwelling on the horrors of the unknown is destructive, but something our society seems to foster.

Bill: The saddest consequence of this negative anticipation is that parents may well drive their children to antisocial behavior of some sort. I remember how you used to tell our children as we left to go to a party, "Don't put any beans up your nose while we're away."

Ruth: They knew that was a family joke.

Bill: Then why do they call Hazel "Bean Nose"?

Ruth: Back on the track, you nut. When disaster strikes, worry ceases and planning for correction begins. In dealing with our children we should work with them as they are, not as our fears lead us to imagine them to be. A desire for a new dress doesn't necessarily indicate that a daughter has no respect for money, is shallow and superficial, is concerned only with appearances, and will be asking for a $1,000 wardrobe next year. She may just want a new dress.

Bill: I think our point is that we must give our children credit for meaning well and show them that we're on their side.

Ruth: At the same time, we must provide them with guidance and support in the direction we want them to take.

Bill: Are there any special considerations for two-career families?

Ruth: I don't think they differ very much from other families as far as children are concerned—except that parents with two successful careers may be more adequate adult models for their children.

Bill: Yes, but those careers are obtained only with great investment of time and effort. Parents should be careful to balance their career investment of time with time at home with the children. And they should be sure that the tension or irritability that arises from their profession does not carry over to their relations with the children.

Ruth: Yes. They should be patient with the underachiever, too, because their very success often intimidates a well-meaning child, who may feel beaten before he starts.

Bill: Still, success breeds success, and two successful careers can be a real asset in dealing with children, who grow up expecting to do well—as your mother convinced you you would do.

Ruth: I've been fortunate in my mother and my children. I hope others can have some of the good times from generation to generation that we've had.

6

Friendship
and
Business

EVEN for people with a happy marriage and two careers, friendship is an essential part of life. For those of us in managerial positions, organizational patterns determine many of our relationships, and these form the working community that gives us a sense of permanence and solidarity. As Andrew M. Greeley points out in *The Friendship Game,* "The key decision-making positions in the corporate bureaucracies must now be occupied not by individuals but rather by problem-solving teams. . . . For such a decision-making team to function well there has to be some kind of basic trust among its members."*

As valuable as this corporate unit may be, it still doesn't satisfy our private need for friendship. Beyond the business and the marriage lies

The Friendship Game (Garden City, New York: Doubleday, 1970), p. 162.

our need to establish continuing one-to-one relationships that support us in our private life and in our work. These friendships will eventually become part of the two-career marriage, but they start in individual ventures. Even when we meet potential friends as a couple, we respond to them individually, deciding independent of each other whether we will include them in our friendship circle.

How we decide, in the midst of the doubts and worries created by our high-tension professional life, who will become part of our friendship community is a complex problem that begins in group activity, moves to solitary analysis, and returns finally to our two-career marriage. In this chapter we will see how important it is to have friends we trust, people who accept us in spite of our weaknesses.

GROUP NEEDS

Some of our friendship needs are initially gratified by fraternal organizations of like-minded people. Service clubs are a good example. Gray had worked in an engineering consulting firm for five years and had begun to dislike many of his co-workers. His naturally competitive spirit and a somewhat aggressive professionalism made him impatient with less qualified associates. A friend asked him to join the local Rotary club, and he laughingly replied, "All I need is another group responsibility." But he joined.

In this group he discovered intelligent professionals from other organizations who were not in overt competition with him and who wished him well. The attendance requirements and the general intellectual interest of the programs satisfied some of his need for community. He developed a brotherly pride in his group. He had enjoyed his college fraternity and missed the fellowship he had known there. Rotary provided him with this sizable support group again.

The gratification Gray received from his weekly fellowship influenced his behavior at work. Although he was still brutally competitive, he was able to separate that urge from his personal relations with the people in the office. His increased good humor probably gained him more than his earlier open antagonism.

Like service clubs, churches immediately give you a common bond with other members. Even if you belong to one congregation, you have the sense of solidarity that comes from knowing that everywhere in the world there are others who share your creed. Unlike service clubs, churches offer membership to everyone in the family. They also offer activities for diverse age groups. There are church scout groups, basketball teams, theater parties, and retirement colonies.

Interest groups—from sailing clubs to investment clubs—are another source of fellowship. Interest groups are diverse enough to get you away from the rest of the family or to permit family involvement. They are structured though not binding, so that you can drop out when you lose interest.

Interest groups constitute a large part of managerial society. Agnes, for example, goes to her investment club on Monday nights, where she talks to people with whom she has no relationship other than their common investments. On Tuesday she goes to her health club after work. There she swims and plays racquet ball in facilities provided by the club. Later in the week she makes plans for a ski trip with her husband through their ski club.

Her husband goes to his weaving class on Wednesday nights and to his Spanish club on Thursday nights. On the weekends, when they're not skiing, they take their children to the country club for dinner. There they see people whom they know only through their frequent dining at the club. After dinner the children play together while their parents gather for bridge.

These groups bring people with common interests together so that conversational topics are ready-made and fellowship selection automatic. The inner diversity of interest groups allows a high degree of personal choice as to the investment of time and money.

The great danger of these organizations—fraternal, religious, and common interest—is that they can become burdens for us. If we begin to regard them as duties instead of pleasures, they are not functioning properly. They should provide group fellowship that will decrease our sense of alienation from others and make us feel part of a society that holds common beliefs. If these groups cease doing that, we should withdraw or change our attitude toward them.

Such groups have another danger, perhaps more serious than the first one. They can become divisive rather than uniting. Fraternal groups, for example, may draw together to the exclusion of others. Although this cliquishness may seem gratifying, it is also limiting.

When groups separate us from other people, we must examine our allegiances to see if we are not distorting the proper function of group fellowship. If our groups show signs of fostering a sense of artificial superiority, we can work to turn the organization toward a healthier course or we can drop our membership.

INDIVIDUAL NEEDS

Although necessary for sociability, groups do not completely fill our friendship needs. Group association gives us a sense of community, but within that community we gradually make distinctions. We find special people with whom we usually sit at lunch, people to whom we talk after a swim, people we invite over for a drink when the committee work is finished. Within our groups we permit people varying degrees of intimacy. Some stop at our front door, some come into the living room or the kitchen, and a few are permitted a view of the basement storeroom.

Different personalities have different friendship needs, but no one is complete in himself. We all want someone we can trust who will be honest with us, sympathize with us, and rejoice with us when the occasion demands it. As Cora Du Bois expresses it in her essay "The Gratuitous Act": "Friendship is a universal human phenomenon . . . , a relationship whatever its form and function, that occurs in all societies."*

This natural urge is never satisfied by group fellowship alone, even though our club may honor us with special recognition on our birthday and give us an "Outstanding Member of the Year Award" for achieving the goals of the group. Although corporate existence sometimes obscures this individual need, it is still present in most of us.

In grade school our world was the classroom we inhabited, and we looked up and down the rows of pupils to choose someone to be our daily companion. As busy people in two-career marriages, we now have numerous friendship possibilities. These possibilities range from conventional social relations to more productive and gratifying forms of friendship.

*The Compact: Selected Dimensions of Friendship, ed. Elliot Leyton (Toronto: University of Toronto Press, 1974), p. 15.

CONVENTIONAL INTIMACY

Conventional intimacy forms approximately 90 percent of our interpersonal exchanges in adult life. Although conventional relationships are professionally and socially valuable, we should not expect to derive our highest personal gratification from them. They are restricted to superficial pleasantries—those habitual responses that make personal relationships agreeable. But we can't demand more of these relationships than they offer, or we will become disillusioned about friendship. Here are some typical kinds of conventional intimacy.

Neighbors

We maintain pleasant relationships in the neighborhood partly because we restrict our interchanges to social amenities. We say a few words across the fence, maybe have a drink together on the weekends, or even go for a round of golf. In this conventional form of intimacy, we must beware of giving wrong impressions.

Henry and Phyllis lived in a suburban area where the neighbors' lawns ran together in uninterrupted greenery down the block. For the first three years they were on equally pleasant terms with those around them. During the third year they discovered that the couple out their backdoor and across the other side of the block were good bridge players. They got in the habit of running over on Saturday afternoons for a few hands of bridge. Since the block was a long one, they didn't want to walk all the way around, so they cut through the backyard of their next-door neighbor and went in their bridge-playing neighbor's backdoor. After about two months, they noticed that their next-door neighbor stopped speaking to them when they met on the street. One day workmen came and put up a six-foot wooden fence around their neighbor's backyard.

Only after the fence was up and the damage done did Henry and Phyllis come to understand the resentment that had been building up against them because they had a special relationship with the bridge-playing neighbors. By failing to maintain minimum conventional intimacy with all their neighbors, they damaged their immediate home environment.

We can deplore the pettiness of people, but we have to live with it, too. Henry and Phyllis should have avoided doing anything slightly offensive if they were going to play favorites in the neighborhood. The next-door neighbors actually thought they were reacting to Henry and Phyllis' trespassing—which, of course, they were. But if Henry and Phyllis had been coming over to talk to them, they would have regarded it as a pleasant intrusion rather than as an irritation. The jealousy offended, not the trespassing.

In general, we must guard private neighborhood relationships carefully. If they cease to be conventional and become productive ones, they may cause trouble. We begin by being pleasantly communicative, and soon we can't work in the garden without having a neighbor hanging over the fence talking to us the entire time we're trying to decide whether to leave the rose bush where it is or move it.

Even more threatening to our privacy is the drop-in visitor. When Doris and Chip first moved into their neighborhood, the older woman next door called on them and they invited her to stay for tea. She told them her life history, to which they listened with polite exclamations of feigned interest. Had they been more sophisticated in the ways of suburban loneliness, they would have begun building their defenses immediately. As it was, they took an interest in the woman and invited her back for supper.

After that, their home life was not their own. Nearly every evening Mrs. Todd sat at their kitchen table while Doris and Chip were trying to prepare supper. Before long Doris developed a tension headache when she drove home from work. She knew the cause, but she didn't know how to handle it. Even her relationship with Chip was affected. Somehow they began snapping at each other because of their suppressed resentment over Mrs. Todd.

The only way to handle such overfriendliness is to freeze it out. They should have said to her, "I'm sorry, but we're tired tonight. Why don't you come back another time?" The third or fourth such rejection would have cooled Mrs. Todd off and kept Chip and Doris from feeling helpless in the face of these attacks on their privacy. If we want to stay in control of our home lives, we have to preserve a reasonable amount of distance in these physically close neighborhood situations.

Co-workers

In our public life the equivalent of a neighbor is the co-worker, who is also part of our environment by necessity rather than choice. The bond of shared space is a strong one, but it doesn't guarantee unanimity of opinion or taste. As a matter of fact, the co-worker, far more than the neighbor, is likely to grow jealous, since competition is implicit in this professional relationship.

Helga, who was striving to get ahead in her career, was lonely because of a bad marriage. She chose to confide in Sally, with whom she had coffee every morning at work. Sally was a good listener. She encouraged Helga to unburden herself and occasionally made suggestions for improving Helga's private life. They laughed a lot about the others in their office who did not seem to find the warm relationship that Helga and Sally shared.

For two years Helga was passed over for a promotion, but at the end of that time Sally was made a branch manager in an office some distance away—a nice advancement for her. Helga did a lot of thinking about her own failure, but she was happy for Sally, whom she rarely saw, although they still chatted on the phone several times a week. Sally was sympathetic with Helga over her inability to move ahead. "Maybe it's your unhappy home life that affects your work," Sally used to tell Helga. And Helga gradually came to believe it.

When Helga tried to build new friendships at the coffeebreak, she discovered that the others in the office were distant and cool toward her. Hurt, she stopped going to coffee and instead kept a thermos at her desk. When she was not given a promotion after the third year, Helga went in to talk to her manager. "We have been worried about you for several years now," the boss said. "Your work is beyond reproach, but you have a reputation for being hard to get along with. You are standoffish and snobbish, and I'm afraid that other people in the section don't like you. I suppose it's because of your unsatisfactory home life."

Helga went back to her desk and thought about the conversation. She had never mentioned her home life to anyone but Sally. The boss could not have known about her private life from anyone else. As she thought back to the interview, she remembered hearing phrases like Sally's in the boss's mouth. Helga began to suspect that Sally had used Helga's confidence to gain superiority in her career—and it had worked.

Helga called Sally and confronted her with her suspicions. "Don't be silly, Helga," Sally said in her sweetest voice. "You have only yourself to blame. You have never been able to get along with people, and the boss and I were in total agreement from the first that you didn't have what it took to get ahead."

Helga's misunderstanding of her relationship with Sally is an example of the confusion of public and private relationships that sometimes develops among co-workers. Business acquaintances are fine for business, but to expect a competitor for advancement to sacrifice that opportunity out of loyalty to a friend is an expectation frequently unsatisfied. While we can be friendly with co-workers, we should not let special relationships separate us from the others in our immediate professional environment.

It is possible to select friends from among our neighbors and co-workers, but Helga erred in mistaking a conventional relationship for a productive one. She thought that she was developing a private intimacy when Sally was only developing her career. A friendship, as distinguished from an acquaintanceship, is built on mutual trust. In the Sally-Helga relationship only Helga was trusting. In the next section we will examine ways of making sure that friendships are reciprocal.

Social Equals

Outside the neighborhood and the professional sphere we meet many people. In political groups, social affairs, and church, lodge, or alumni meetings, we interact with congenial people who share many of our attitudes and values. Most of the time we chat pleasantly when we meet without saying anything profound or memorable. Once in a while we talk with someone we really like, but the conversation doesn't lead to anything beyond the single encounter.

As useful socially or professionally as these relationships are, they too have to be classified as conventional ones. They reassure us, the way larger group relationships do, that we are part of a larger fellowship of believers in a certain way of life. When we are with people who talk the same way we do and react to social situations the same way, we are at ease.

In all three kinds of individual relationships—neighbor, co-worker, and social equal—we reinforce our convictions and come away enriched by that reassurance. Sometimes, though, we can mistakenly assume that a few similarities indicate more agreement than they actually do. We should not expect an electric mixer to run a motor boat, nor should we expect a conventional friendship to propel us through our deepest emotional waters. Neighbors are wonderful when we need to borrow a cup of sugar or a power saw. But that conventional relationship should not be expected to take the strain of a larger task than that.

FROM CONVENTIONAL TO PRODUCTIVE

Productive intimacy requires more effort and time than conventional relations. No one has time, before retirement, for more than a limited amount of productive intimacy, because it requires both thought and constant upkeep. Still, we need several people we can trust, people who will go out of their way for us—as we will for them—not because they feel they should but because they want to. Productive intimacy permits an open exchange of ideas and is a loving, reciprocal affair.

A number of anthropologists and sociologists have analyzed friendship patterns. Robert Paine, who has written extensively on friendship, gives numerous indications of the requirements of friendship in his essay "In Search of Friendship: An Exploratory Analysis in 'Middle-Class' Culture."* Using his research as our starting point, we devised the following test for productive friendship.

Friendship Analysis

1. Do you have several people whom you see frequently simply because you want to rather than out of professional or social necessity?
2. At large parties do you usually talk to one person more than you circulate from group to group?
3. Do you engage regularly in activities with another person—fishing, tennis, bridge, and so on—rather than in group sports such as softball?
4. With special family or professional problems would you talk to someone you know rather than seeking help from a counselor or professional superior?
5. Do you know someone with whom you would discuss any aspect

*Published in *Man*, New Series 4:4, December 1969, pp. 505–524.

of your life without fear that he would tell somebody else your problem?

Explanation

Secure Intimacy. If you answered yes to all five questions, you already have a healthy degree of intimacy in your life. You are capable of productive friendships and are achieving a high degree of satisfaction from them. All you have to do now is to recognize their value and maintain them in their present satisfactory state.

Normal Intimacy. If you answered yes to three or four questions, you are in the median group of adult Americans. You probably spend more time than you want in conventional group activities; but you have managed to save enough of your energy and time to cultivate a few intimate companions. You would probably enjoy your private life more if you could eliminate some of your conventional relationships and give more time to those productive ones that you have.

Insecurity. If you answered yes to fewer than three questions, you probably spend much of your time feeling apprehensive and lonely. Everyone needs some productive relationships that build trust and confidence. Group relationships alone are not adequate. Even strong, healthily self-sufficient people derive some of their health from productive intimacies.

From the groups you now frequent, select several people to whom you are naturally attracted. After you have made sure they are available and trustworthy, try talking openly with them about things that matter to you. Emptiness and self-doubt come from too much dependence on conventional relationships. The following section suggests ways to move from conventional intimacies to productive ones.

LEVELS OF PRODUCTIVE INTIMACY

In our daily group encounters we meet many people who are capable of productive intimacy. If we are greedy, we try to channel too many of these into productive friendships and end up with muddled human relationships—broken promises, missed appointments, personality conflicts, parties that don't come off. If we are shy and hesitant, we yearn for the kind of warm exchanges we see in others, often feeling jealousy and resentment. All of us are in control, though, of both our private life and our public one. We can limit or expand our stages of intimacy as we see fit.

We must begin with a realistic understanding of the demands of productive intimacy. When we are beginning a family and a career, we have to put most of our energy and time into these extremely important jobs. Since only a very small percentage of our time is available for nonessential activity, we may have to depend at this stage on the less demanding, conventional forms of friendship.

Later, when the children are making lives for themselves and we are in control of our jobs, we have more time for productive intimacies. In this second stage of development we may overreact to our new freedom. We should not undertake more productive friendships than we can easily handle. Our friendship time is still limited by professional and family demands, and even now too many close friends can be like too many martinis—after the first two we feel good, but after a few more we feel sick.

Only at the end of our professional lives, when retirement gives us more freedom than before, can we happily investigate extended intimacies. Then we can choose whether to withdraw into our own family or to expand to other kinds of fellowship.

In retirement, when we have the leisure to cultivate intimate friendships, our decreased group activities may limit the field of selection. Unless we make an effort to associate with other people at the same stage of development, we are likely to feel lonely and neglected. Our younger friends are still pursuing their careers with groups that are now part of our past. During this period of transition, we may need to turn again to conventional group associations—churches, interest groups, and fraternal orders. Through these we can build special relationships that may become as rich in intimacy as those of our high school days, when the world was before us.

At all three stages in our life, we can pursue many different levels of productive intimacy. These are as intricate as life itself, but we can begin to make some finer distinctions by naming a few.

Coffee Companion

In Anglo-Saxon times, when our language was beginning to emerge from its Germanic background, there was a word that meant "hearth companion." In the third and fourth centuries, when the warriors gathered at night with their mead cups around the great stone fireplaces and listened to the wolves howling outside in the snow, this special name referred to a special relationship. Although we are no longer plagued by wolves, we still have the same need for special persons with whom we can draw aside and drink. In a managerial setting, this is the coffee companion.

The coffee companion relationship can be the first stage of increasing intimacy. It doesn't have to be, of course. We can drink coffee with some people every morning for five years and never get to know them more than casually. Coffee drinking is the kind of ritual occasion, though, that can provide an opportunity for a productive relationship.

Our coffee companions frequently grow into closer friends. Sometimes, though, when a person's professional or personal situation changes—a promotion, a divorce, a transfer—the relationship also changes. At times of drastic change in our lives or that of our coffee companion we need to make sure that the relationship hasn't changed too.

After seven years of coffee companionship, one man began knifing his friend in the back because he had been promoted to section chief. "I hate administrators," the turncoat companion said to a co-worker, "and I told him so. I just said, 'Now that you're a manager, I probably won't be able to be your friend.'" At least in this case, when the relationship changed, the friend was honest enough to say so.

Playmate

If coffee companionship is productive, it moves to the playmate level. In your coffee conversations you find someone who shares your interests. One day you find yourselves taking the afternoon off together. Or you stop for a drink together after work.

Tim was thirty-seven and Jake forty-two when they met. Both had advanced to supergrades in the Department of Transportation, where they were making about the same amount of money. Although they had worked in the same building for many years, they were on different floors and their duties didn't overlap. They began talking one day at lunch when they had to share a table in the crowded cafeteria. They compared notes about their superiors, careful not to introduce themselves to each other so that they could talk more freely.

They enjoyed talking so much that they met the next day for lunch.

Before long they were having lunch together when they didn't have other appointments. Each told his wife that he had finally met one other person who wasn't one of those groveling sycophants. This person was both smart and nice—a rare combination. Tim's wife laughed and said, "You mean he agrees with you." Tim admitted that was probably part of Jake's charm.

In the course of their conversations they arranged to go out one weekend with their wives. To their dismay, their wives did not take to each other. At lunch the next week they coyly felt each other out about the disappointing evening. "Oh, hell," Jake said. "Let's not let our wives come between us."

One spring day they were talking about an article on sailing in Chesapeake Bay that they had read in *Potomac Magazine*. Both admitted they had always wanted to sail but had never learned how. "Let's arrange for lessons," Tim suggested.

That afternoon Jake telephoned around and found out where they could get sailing lessons. Every Saturday morning that spring they were down at the marina. Within a year they had bought a sailboat together and spent their spare time reading up on riggings. After they had been sailing together for about two years, the wives began to feel left out and asked their husbands if they could come along. The common interest brought the four of them together, and when they sailed from Washington to Savannah one weekend, all four had a good time.

This playmate level of intimacy, growing out of the coffee companion level, transcends conversation and moves into cooperative action. You don't have to buy a sailboat to have a playmate, of course. All you need is someone who shares your ideas of a good time. When you find him, don't be hesitant. You've lost nothing if he's not available for a deeper level of intimacy. And if he is available, you've begun an interesting new expansion of your friendship.

Like the coffee companionship, though, the playmate relationship must work both ways. You can play with some people for years and have nothing but a worn-out catcher's mitt to show for the effort. If your games and good times don't show a deepening of your appreciation of each other, you should start finding other playmates.

Buddy

"Buddy"—a word popularized by soldiers in World War I to indicate a special attachment to a kindred spirit—is a suitable term for the third level of intimacy. Another old-fashioned word appropriate for this level is "chum"—the one Tom Swift and Nancy Drew used to describe associates who helped them solve mysteries and do daring feats against the universe.

Your buddies are those who have made it through the first levels of intimacy. This level combines the coffee companion and the playmate with the more demanding role of spiritual supporter and guide. Buddies are emotionally bound up with each other. When one suffers, the other one suffers too; when one is happy, the other's life is brighter.

Few of us have more than one or two buddies at a time, if that many. The strain on our lives of having to accept the burden of another person's fate as well as our own is a sizable one. On the other hand, the sharing of burdens works both ways. When we are in trouble, we have someone outside our family whose sympathy and aid we can count on.

To find buddies we have to go through a good many coffee companions and playmates. Buddies are not put aside and taken up as easily as those people at earlier stages of intimacy. They develop as we establish a growing unity built on previously shared experiences. When we make a commitment to a buddy, it is broken only with some pain on both sides.

Denise liked Lila because she was easy to work with. When Lila was transferred to another city, the two of them sometimes spent weekends together. They talked and shopped, and while they visited each other's houses they were readily accepted almost as part of the family. One day Lila called Denise to tell her that her husband was ill and needed a rest. Denise didn't hesitate. "Why don't you send the kids down to stay with us and go on a trip together," she offered. Lila protested, and so did Denise's husband, but Denise insisted. And it worked out well. That's what being a buddy consists of—sharing each other's total lives and not minding the inconveniences that are likely to arise from the friendship.

Blood Brother

The blood brother level of intimacy is a sort of nonsexual marriage in which the buddy relation is intensified and consciously developed. Few people get this far in their ascent toward total intimacy, but it is the state into which, ideally, the earlier forms evolve. Terms like "soul mate" and "secret sharer" express the spiritual bond that exists at this level.

In earlier cultures the mingling of blood in a ritual ceremony cemented the relationship. We don't go that far, but we can imagine caring about someone outside our family enough to take great risks for him. Even more than that is our anticipation of attaining a childhood ideal—someone so compatible that we can know each other's thoughts even before we speak.

In his short story "The Secret Sharer," Joseph Conrad tells of a sea captain on his first voyage and of a strange fleeing felon who shares with him the secret of almost overwhelming fear at the new responsibility. When we have found someone who is willing to reveal to us what we most fear and when we have joined wordlessly in a struggle against that fear, we are at the place where intimacy is complete.

The blood brother relationship is the ideal toward which we strive. But we can't force it. Few coffee companions or even buddies are ready for the selfless maturity this relationship requires. When we find such a person, we should strive to prove through our loyalty and trust that these relationships are worth attaining.

PATTERNS OF FRIENDSHIP

To achieve the kind of intimacy that enriches our public and private lives simultaneously, we have to "see with parted eye," as Hermia says in Shakespeare's *A Midsummer Night's Dream*. We have to be unselfconsciously receptive to new possibilities of human interchange but cooly rational about our needs and our own qualifications for friendship. The way we develop friendships is conditioned by our background and experiences—the preferences, tastes, disappointments, and successes that inform our expectations. Here are several of the most common patterns of friendship selection.

The Ghetto Pattern

The most common way of choosing friends is along insular lines—selecting people from the closed world around us. Those in the ghetto associate with others there because they are alike—in location, background, and ambition. They don't look beyond these possibilities because in a limited way they are satisfied with what is present there.

Sometimes, though, a nagging dissatisfaction results from such limited friendship. The selection process has been too restricted, the inbreeding too intense.

As valuable as this type of friendship is, the pattern cannot always be trusted as a desirable selection process. Miriam worked in the secretarial pool of a large company. Along with fifty others she spent her days typing from the tapes that came down to her. When she went for coffee, the talk was generally about the tapes, the other typists, and the people who, somewhere outside their tape-bound ghetto, decided what they were going to do each day.

Although Miriam was intelligent, she had little ambition. She was working because her family needed extra money and because she was bored at home with two children. She was bored at work, too, but it was easier for her to spend her time drinking coffee with the other typists than to do anything else.

Several of her co-workers asked her and her husband Joel to do things on the weekends—come over for pizza, go bowling, or see a movie. Joel was busy with his own career, but he went along uncomplainingly to play with Miriam's friends.

After several years Miriam and Joel grew bored with this ghetto existence. Miriam whined a lot and expected sympathy from Joel. Joel, looking for excitement, began a dreary affair with one of the typists who worked with Miriam. When Miriam found out about the affair, she was hurt and confused. "I thought you were my friend, Sherry," she said to her co-worker.

"I'm as much your friend as I ever was. Joel was bored and so was I," Sherry said. "You've listened to stories of my affairs with married men before and never said anything about it. I didn't think you'd care."

Miriam's disappointment in her friendship resulted from her passive acceptance of what was readily available. She settled for ghetto narrowness instead of looking in other areas for people with whom she could have begun an exciting excursion into intimacy. Miriam should have known herself well enough to see that a superficial life of killing time would grow stale. She and Joel needed friends with more depth than the ones Miriam found for them.

Although work is a normal place to develop friends, it is not the only place. If we are not like the rest of our associates, we are going to have to find another way to get started on the intimacy route. We should range freely before we make our final friendship selection. To settle for the closest and most convenient people can lead to unfortunate mismatches. If we know ourselves before we start knowing our friends, we'll be better able to shake loose from ghetto restrictions and fulfill our needs from a larger area.

The Army Pattern

The army is the opposite of the ghetto—people are constantly on the move. Army friendships develop quickly because of the temporary nature of assignments. People will soon move on to a new post, where they will find a new set of friends to replace the old ones. In each assignment they can go instantly to the officer's club, the NCO club, the dayroom, or the chapel. Any of these places offers wide friendship possibilities.

Many of our friendships are of the army type. We commit ourselves to them fervently while we are with a certain organization—high school, college, a particular company. But when we move on, we go to a new situation that offers replacement friendships. When we leave our old friends, we make promises of writing and plans for visiting. But we know that at our new post we will have to devote our limited time to developing new friends rather than maintaining old ones.

Army friendship is not necessarily good or bad. That's just the way it is—instant attraction and involvement followed by instant detachment and reinvolvement. The strength of such friendships is their energy. When you know that life will pass you by, you don't loiter on the threshold of a relationship but push right into it. You live fully for the moment rather than spinning out your time in vain regrets for other times and places.

The army pattern teaches the importance of initiative in developing friendships. If you are part of a corporate community where transfers are frequent, you have to capitalize on the virtues of the army pattern. If you see someone who looks promising on your new post, make a strong initial bid for the friendship. Do not take rejection as a personal slur; usually it is a matter of time and availability. People may be too busy to make room for you. But as a newcomer, you have the advantage of your novelty. Coming from another world to this one, you offer news and views that will enliven the old group.

In the army pattern the fervor of friendship is stronger than it is in a more stable society. You are part of a large corporate community in which people share many of the same attitudes and values. Your strength comes from being not so much in competition as in joint collaboration to preserve your psychic health in the impersonal organization that shoves you from place to place.

The Barroom Pattern

The barroom pattern of friendship focuses on the pursuit of pleasure. Barroomers have a good time, but they don't anticipate lasting intimacy.

Oscar was introduced to his local barroom set shortly after he started working as night editor for a large Los Angeles newspaper. Although he had held several positions on smaller papers, this was his first executive position on a city paper. Since he worked nights, he usually had to drive home about 2:00 A.M. For the first month he was awake until five or six because he was so keyed up from work that he couldn't go to bed immediately after getting home.

Oscar mentioned this problem to one of the people in his section and was invited to go out after work for a relaxing nightcap. He got in the habit of joining ten or twelve members of the editorial staff every night after work. They drank until four or five in the morning, then had breakfast together before going home. Oscar got to know the favorite spots and was soon putting in a good deal of money and time on these nightly tours.

Before long he became romantically involved with one of the women in the group. Oscar thought he was in love with her, but he soon learned that he was only one of a string of men in her life. Hurt by this news, Oscar began looking around for a friend to confide in. His nightly companions, with whom he had been drinking for a year, smiled at him condescendingly and said, "Don't take it seriously, Oscar. It's all in fun. Go back home to your wife till you find somebody else."

Oscar withdrew from the group and became so lonely that he began drinking heavily and having difficulties at his job. His mistake was in expecting a position in the barroom set to lead to any reciprocal concern or emotional development. Like the other patterns of friendship, this one is useful only if you know what to expect from it.

The Hand-Mixed Pattern

We are inclined to expect a single satisfactory pattern for friendship. We accept the one that our parents and childhood friends gave us. Even though it may have been consistently unsatisfactory, we continue working with the pattern we know. But we need not tie ourselves to any specific pattern. Instead, we should make the most of the personalities around us, mixing our needs with what others are capable of offering. When we do, we will move through degrees of intimacy to a point where we know other people and have the pleasure of being known and understood by them.

"Understanding" is probably the key word in friendship. It comes from wide experience in plodding through difficult moments and getting past individual differences. But at the end of the struggle lies the realization that we are able to share the joy and sorrow of being human with someone else. Once we achieve that understanding with someone, we will find it easier to develop friendships all along the line.

FRIENDSHIP FOR COUPLES

So far we have talked primarily about friendship as if it were an individual matter. Most of us in two-career marriages also need to think of friendship in terms of couples. Since our free time is so limited, we can use it more efficiently if we see friends together as well as separately.

Friendship is difficult enough to attain at a one-to-one level. To find two couples who are compatible is more than twice as difficult. And to find another family in which the children mesh with the adults is a rare discovery indeed. In spite of their rarity, such multiple relationships can develop.

Multiple friendships usually begin individually. Most of the time the husbands or wives of the two friends—assuming both couples are happily married—also enjoy the same things and will like each other. Sometimes, though, a certain competitiveness or antagonism has to be overcome before a solid basis for friendship can be established. Tim and Jake, who began their sailing careers on Chesapeake Bay, illustrate this point. By the time they introduced their wives to each other, their friendship was so firmly established that the women felt pressured into a relationship over which they had little choice. Their immediate resentment was a natural assertion of their independence. Only later were the women able to become friends.

Generally, the second member of a couple should be introduced rather soon after the initial friendship develops so that all four people can build intimacy together. At the playmate stage, for example, it is easy to turn tennis singles into doubles. If two women enjoy an afternoon of shopping together, they can meet the men for dinner downtown so that part of their leisure time is spent as couples.

Once you begin a friendship as a couple, your natural desire to share it will help expand to family experiences. Camping and picnics are an easy way to get started. Fishing, weekend trips, skiing, and other group activities can be adjusted to family needs. The best environment for family fellowship is one in which no one feels pressured into a close relationship with anybody else. If everyone is having a good time together, the general mood is likely to carry the hesitant ones along.

A tradition of good friendship is valuable for two-career couples and their children. The family that tries to maintain a consistently high-pressured professional atmosphere is likely to crack under the strain. The development of close friendships is a valuable expression of your social needs. Intimate personal relationships grow naturally if you take the time to look for the early signs of friendship and cultivate the potential companionship available there.

The Joneses Talk About Friendship

Ruth: I think the main point we make in this chapter is that if people aren't satisfied with their friends and associates there are ways to build more satisfactory relationships.

Bill: I agree. But I hope our analysis of friendship won't simply make people dissatisfied with the friends they already have.

Ruth: It's true that too much analysis can kill a friendship, but we were mainly concerned in the chapter with not confusing conventional relations with real friendship.

Bill: I suppose you might say we're arguing for an active program of Friendship Transformation. What we hope is that people will develop an increased interest in productive personal relationships rather than sacrificing them for more superficial or immediate gratifications.

Ruth: Realism in no way implies cynicism, and a realistic assessment of our relationships with associates should lead to an increased enjoyment of those relations— or a modification of them.

Bill: We're assuming that everyone is capable of friendship and that it is an essential ingredient of a full life for two-career couples. Have we ever known people who didn't need friends?

Ruth: I'm sure you're thinking of one man who informed us that he and his wife didn't need friends. Subsequent events proved him wrong, but they also proved he had good friends he could rely on.

Bill: In other words, sometimes the friendship process works quite adequately even if we're unaware that it's working.

Ruth: It wouldn't have worked for this man if he hadn't done his part. He put in a lot of time with people of similar interests and values who had a large capacity for friendship. An expert violinist has practiced his technique until it is automatic. He may not be able to explain each move or even be aware he is making it, but he continues to perform competently. Our friend, even in his assertion of independence and self-reliance, had cultivated so many friends that he continued doing so in his period of personal rebellion.

Bill: Sometimes in our more depressed moments you and I say we don't have any friends. Do you think that is a natural feeling for busy couples?

Ruth: That statement says more about how little time and thought we've given other people than about the way they feel toward us.

Bill: What do you mean?

Ruth: That when we say we don't have any friends we've been devoting our time and attention to ourselves. It's possible to be too busy for friendship. Each couple has to determine what its values in this area are.

Bill: In other words, the old maxim "To have friends you must be one" is still valid?

Ruth: As long as we examine the situation realistically to determine if it's mutual. But we'll sacrifice friendship with a couple if we don't take the time to respond to their overtures. Nobody's going to continue knocking on our door forever.

Bill: So if we don't have the friends we want it's because we've put something else first on our priority list. I'll agree with that.

7

Social
Life
and
Recreation

THE way two-career couples manage their leisure time is one indication of their professional and private success. If we are dissatisfied at work or at home, the maladjustment will be apparent in our social and recreational patterns before it is evident in other areas of our lives.

Eddie was the manager of a brokerage firm in his hometown when he and Libby married. Libby worked as a receptionist in her father's water softener company. A large part of their recreational and social life continued as it had before they married. Eddie belonged to a softball league, and Libby played cards with the women she had known in high school. On weekends they went to movies with friends and then had them over afterward.

The only change in their social pattern after marriage was that now Libby prepared the refreshments instead of her mother. She didn't mind, even when Eddie decided that he ought to have the agents and their wives over for a picnic in the summer and a cocktail party at Christmas. That was what married life was about. Eddie and Libby were taking their place in the business community the way their parents had done, and they accepted the responsibility as part of their job. They still had plenty of time to watch TV and talk on the phone to old friends.

Then Eddie was offered a job with a much larger agency in the state capital, two hundred miles away. The new salary was so attractive that Eddie couldn't pass it up, even though it meant leaving family and old friends. Libby resented having to give up her job in the family business to satisfy Eddie's ambition. "You'll find another job," Eddie said. "You've had good experience, and we need to get away from our families."

For the first few months in their new home Libby was busy getting settled. Her mother came to help her decorate the house, and they had a good time together. After six months, the house was ready and the relatives gone. Eddie was busier at the office than he had ever been. He brought work home with him and sometimes worked until after Libby was asleep. Libby was bored and lonely. "You can watch just so much TV," she wrote her mother, "and then you begin talking like a character out of Love of Life."

Libby found a job with a produce company in the invoice office. She worked with shipping receipts all day and rarely had any contact with other people. After work she wanted to go out to eat or to a movie, but Eddie was usually too busy or too tired. He spent most of his days with customers at lunch, and he was ready for a quiet evening at home when work was over.

Libby began to resent Eddie's job. When he asked her to have a party for the brokers and their wives, Libby snapped at him, "They're your friends; you have the party." This response was so unlike the woman he had married that Eddie said nothing more and decided to have a dinner party at a restaurant instead of bringing his staff home.

After he made the arrangements for the party and invited the people, he told Libby about his plans. She was enraged. "Why don't you tell me what you're going to do? Don't you think I enjoy spending our money too? If you're going to rent out a restaurant, I might as well have the fun of selecting the place and the menu." Although Eddie tried to explain that he wanted to save her from extra work, she was so angry that she refused to go to the party.

Eddie was embarrassed and resentful at having to explain Libby's absence. Although he tried to be understanding, he made no more offers to take Libby out, and their social life soon took separate directions. Eddie spent his free time with the men at the office, and Libby stayed home, unable to find friends or activities that were interesting to her. After several years of loneliness and squabbling, Libby left Eddie and went back to her job with her father.

Libby and Eddie's experiences illustrate most of the problems that can arise for two-career couples in their social and recreational life. They didn't understand that social needs shift in the course of a marriage and that they must occasionally reevaluate this area, where they are free to make their own choices.

Libby and Eddie never graduated from the courtship pattern of recreation. Their social life would have probably become boring even if Eddie had decided to stay in his hometown. In their new situation, the difference in their jobs led to different social needs. Since neither recognized these needs, they grew apart, never taking the time to explore the possibilities for successful use of leisure time in two-career marriages.

USES OF LEISURE TIME

Your leisure is divided into those activities that are required, or at least useful, for advancement in your public life and those that give you personal gratification. You have control over both areas, and the way you control them can determine whether the two careers in your family are rewarding or destructive to your relationship. Here are examples of both.

Professional Use of Leisure

Maggie and Bill were both deeply committed to their careers. Maggie was senior communications specialist for a cosmetics company. She supervised a dozen public relations agents who worked to maintain pleasant relationships between the company staff and the clients. Bill had a small engineering consulting firm that employed three people. Shortly after they married, they saw that they were going to spend much of their social life apart from each other. Their evenings and weekends were not their own. Bill took his customers to dinner, and Maggie went to cocktail parties with dinner and a meeting afterward.

These professional "social" activities satisfied their need for companionship so completely that, when they were home together, they put on T-shirts and cutoffs, opened a can of sardines, and sat around reading back issues of *Newsweek* without talking to each other.

Outsiders asked them how they could get along with so little time together. Their answer: "We have the best times together—doing nothing." Their rare moments alone were a wise investment of their limited nonprofessional social time. Their professions both required intense social activity; and since they were good at their jobs, they accepted the social responsibilities willingly. They also liked each other, but they didn't fool themselves into thinking that they had to pile on more social activities simply because they didn't go to parties together. Their private inactivity compensated for their frantic pace at work.

Maggie and Bill are unusual in that they are aware of the favorable balance that two-career couples must maintain in their private and public lives. Everyone has professional responsibilities that may seem to be social occasions but that are actually professional choices. As long as we count them as part of our jobs—and part of our lives as well—we can determine how much of our social life we can adjust to make room for them.

The professional social activities that Maggie and Bill engage in are common among business couples. You will not find soul mates at office parties and business lunches, but you will develop improved departmental relationships and happier clients. Any personal benefits derived from business socializing are by-products of the occasion.

Other activities that we engage in because we hold a certain position are not so clearly business-related. Serving on the United Fund board, going to church suppers, playing ball for the company team, or having business associates over for dinner—even though only indirectly necessary for professional advancement—must be excluded from our personal recreation time. After all, these too enhance our public image for business purposes.

Private Use of Leisure

When we have finished doing what is necessary for our professional advancement, we should still have some time left over for ourselves. With this we chart out a program to revitalize ourselves physically and emotionally. Some regular physical exercise and some other release from tension—either a hobby, socializing with friends, or a solitary activity such as reading—are the minimum requirements for a private recreational program. Even though the rest of our time may be prescribed for us by economic necessity, one small portion has to be ours alone.

How we use this time depends on the kind of professional life we lead. If we are with people all day long, as Maggie and Bill are, we will probably want some solitary activity during our time off. If we have few human contacts in our work, we will need more social activity and fewer solitary pursuits. If ours is a desk job, we will want physical exercise, and if we are physically active in our work, we may enjoy a quiet, sit-down hobby such as stamp or coin collecting.

Our natural interests are often reflected in our choice of profession. Thus librarians read for relaxation and professional ball players run track. These natural inclinations cannot be disputed. Still, we should consciously apportion our leisure time so that we have a balanced program of physical and intellectual activity.

Leisure activities are anything we choose to do in our free time, even things that others might consider work. Thus, for the office-bound manager, mowing the yard every Saturday morning may be a wise use of leisure time, and that has to be counted as recreational effort, because he chooses to do it rather than pay someone else to do it. The same is true of financial dealings. We can choose to spend our free time studying the market and investing in stocks and commodities. Although this can be a money-making activity, it is still an elective recreational pursuit. Sometimes making money can be one of the most pleasant uses of leisure time.

Some of our leisure will probably be devoted to the family. Reading to the children, cooking something special, and even washing curtains are recreational activities since, technically, we could survive without them. Our attitude toward these tasks will be improved when we realize that we can indeed choose to do them or neglect them.

Most of us get so accustomed to achieving professionally that we strive to achieve even around the house, a place designed for our comfort. Home becomes a torture chamber when we are constantly looking for ways to improve it. The unpainted garage and the dirty cupboards are not disgraceful. If we prefer a picnic to a paint job, we should choose the picnic.

Group sports, family life, household chores, and simply loafing are equally acceptable uses of leisure, as long as we choose them freely. We should trust our good judgment in selecting from among these leisure activities to achieve a balanced life. We need to see people? Then we see people. We need solitude? Then we choose solitude.

Successful management of leisure time is knowing that it is totally ours and becoming aware of the possibilities. We should not let pressures from friends or professional demands becloud our understanding of what is right for our own personalities. Wisely used, leisure can become a constructive force in our lives.

PERSONALITY, CAREER, AND LEISURE TIME

By assessing our attitude toward our daily activities, we can better understand our personality needs. Knowing that, we can then develop an appropriate program for our leisure time. Jack and Terri worked out such a program after they realized how much they needed one. Jack, a regional representative for a textbook company, spent most of his time driving around the West Coast talking to his field editors and college professors who might write texts for his company. Terri worked as a computer programmer in the basement of a large insurance building only a few miles from their home. Within this marriage are the two extremes of managerial type. Jack managed people and Terri managed numbers; Jack was person-related and Terri was object-related.

They both liked their jobs, but when they came to us, their marriage was not a happy one. They didn't know the cause, but part of their problem was their different needs for leisure time. Their case is typical of many two-career couples who have different jobs and different personalities, but who believe that recreation has to be a cooperative activity.

Terri complained that Jack never took her out to eat or dance, and Jack said that Terri would not leave him at peace when he was at home. He had joined a softball team, not because he liked softball but because it got him out of the house. We worked out a four-step leisure time formula that solved their problem. Many two-career couples may find it useful.

Step 1: Objective Analysis

The first step in adjusting your leisure time is to realize that you need to. It is easy to get in the habit of bickering when you are together, simply because you have nothing more constructive to do with your time and are too tired to do anything else. Unless you know what you want to do when you have time on your hands, you may vent your frustration on each other. Jack and Terri had begun to dislike each other without knowing why.

If you aren't having the kind of fun you used to have together, it is possible that you are bringing an outmoded dating mentality to your marriage. Terri felt that Jack's main purpose in marriage was to act as her escort when she wanted to go out. Jack felt that Terri should still be the coy girl who said, "Oh, you decide what to do. I don't really care. I'll be happy doing whatever you want." But the permanence of their marriage made each of them fearful of threats to their independent use of leisure time. They felt trapped by a sense of responsibility for each other's spare time.

No matter how long you've been married, you begin a study of leisure time by studying your job, which forms the bulk of your daily life. What you do there will help determine what you want to do and need to do with the rest of your time. Jack, who ate a lot of lunches with business acquaintances and spent nights in motels, more than fulfilled his social needs during the week. Terri, on the other hand, was starved for social life because of the solitary nature of her job.

Their analysis began with the realization of this difference in their jobs and thus their widely divergent leisure needs. At first this discovery dismayed them. "Then we're not suited for each other at all," Terri said. But we refused to let her get by with this easy way out of a marriage that was basically sound.

"Let's not draw any conclusions till we've finished all four steps," we suggested. "You don't need to give up hope yet."

Step 2: Subjective Response to Work

Work can have either a generative or degenerative effect on people. In spite of the differences in their jobs, Jack and Terri both had degenerative workweeks. They gave out energy like a battery and needed recharging in the evenings and on the weekends. Both needed a recreational pattern that contrasted with their work pattern. Other personalities, in the same jobs as those Terri and Jack had, might have derived energy from their work. People who find their profession generative often do the same things for recreation that they do at work. The manager of a Howard Johnson's restaurant spends his leisure time planning parties for the weekend. A CPA whose only contact during the week is with his calculator prefers to spend the weekend working on his car or doing crossword puzzles.

What is your own attitude toward work? Do you thrive on the socializing, or is it an aspect of the job that you endure because you find other parts rewarding? Do you enjoy the times when you have to be alone, or do you find your mind wandering into depressing depths?

The answer for most of us is that we need some solitude and some socializing. When we spend long hours at business lunches, we grow disgusted with them; but when we have spent a week and a half alone at our desk writing an annual report, we are starved for company.

Step 3: Ideal Solution

Every couple with divergent leisure time needs should discuss their present job situations and then try to work out their ideal plan for use of leisure time. Jack and Terri needed to sit down together and tell each other how they would have liked to use their free time. According to Terri, all she wanted was a chance once in a while to go out or to have some people over for conversation and laughs. All Jack wanted was to stretch out in front of the TV and watch sports.

Obviously, their ideal solutions conflicted, since Terri's plan included Jack and Jack's excluded Terri. Still, even though their ideals were unattainable, they needed to express to each other just what they wanted. Otherwise, they would not have been able to move on to step 4.

Step 4: Practical Compromise

Having clearly verbalized their ideal solution, Jack and Terri might have continued their conversation this way:

Terri: I haven't seen anybody all week. I'd really like to have some people over tomorrow night—maybe fix some pizza and talk.

Jack: I'd be happy if I didn't see anybody for the next ten years. I've had enough—something every night this week.

Terri: That's fine for you, but what about me?

Jack: Why don't you do something on your own? I've got a game I want to watch on TV.

Terri: Well, why don't we have two or three couples over with the understanding that those who want to watch TV can do that while the rest of us talk?

Jack: I could stand that—but I won't dress up. I won't even shave.

Terri: OK. I'll tell them to wear whatever they have on, and we'll eat pizza and just do nothing.

If a couple talks long enough, they will find something they both enjoy—even if it's separate activities. By working through a conversation like the previous one, Jack and Terri could both have had a good time Sunday night at their party. Jack would have made no effort to prepare for it and would not even have had to change his clothes. Terri could have satisfied her entertainment need by cooking up something special and wearing something exotic. Thus Terri, who was hungry for company, could have made the effort without forcing Jack to take her out.

The practical compromise is always available. It simply assumes that the one who wants the action stirs up action without unsettling the passive member of the couple. Assume a reversal in the Jack and Terri situation. Now Jack wants the party and Terri doesn't. He negotiates for a compromise and concludes by having some people over for hamburgers, which he buys and grills outdoors. Terri has to make no effort and can even excuse herself and go to bed if she gets tired of the guests.

In two-career marriages, the old middle-class rules for entertaining no longer apply. Your life is more important than a party. You make realistic rules that your friends accept, as you accept theirs. These are the only kind of friends to have in a world of limited leisure. Nobody needs a set of judgmental competitors. There are plenty of those at the office.

WORKING AND ENTERTAINING

In liaison marriages the wife prides herself on genteel entertaining that enhances her husband's professional position. Even in two-career marriages, many women still regard the home as *their* responsibility. A certain amount of possessiveness is fine, but two-career couples have a number of choices, one of which is a total sharing of home responsibilities. In joint tenancy you are freed of the burden of defensiveness that accompanies possessiveness. You no longer hear the cries, "What are you doing messing up *my* kitchen?" and "Don't put your feet on *my* coffeetable." When both share responsibility for the kitchen and the coffeetable, the negative attitude disappears.

When two people spend the same amount of time on their jobs, they cannot expect the other to undertake all the responsibility for entertaining. Like the rest of marriage, that has to be shared. Entertainment divides easily into two sorts—the kind you do for professional reasons and the kind you do for fun. You have to be clear about which is which. Although you have to fulfill certain professional obligations, you can be selective about your other social activities. You don't have to have people back to dinner simply because they had you, and you don't have to go to a ballgame with a friend if you don't want to.

By the same token, you must not be resentful if someone doesn't have you back to dinner or refuses to go to a ballgame with you. One couple has not spoken to us for three years because we refused to join their bridge club—the most important thing in their lives. We don't miss their company. The world is full of interesting people, and couples have only themselves to blame if they let other people determine the way they "entertain" themselves.

The most common problem that arises with entertaining is managing to get everything done when it should be done. Every time you invite someone into your house you cannot help feeling some need to pick up a few things and prepare food. Even the most casual entertainment requires effort on somebody's part.

As suggested in the last section, the partner who cares most about a particular party should take primary responsibility for planning and preparation. Still, it is a joint venture, and by talking it through you can sometimes find easier ways of doing things so that the party becomes fun instead of a burden. Suppose that Jack and Terri have now reached a new accord in their attitude toward socializing. With their new sympathy for each other, they come across this social situation:

Jack: We've owed the boss a dinner for over a year now. We've got to have him over.

Terri: You couldn't have picked a worse time. I've got to work overtime for the next month to get things ready for a long-range-planning meeting.

Jack: Well, this isn't something that we can keep putting off.

Terri: He probably doesn't want to come much more than we want to have him. Instead of having a dinner party here, why don't we have him and his wife over for cocktails and then take them to the new Italian restaurant everybody's talking about?

Jack: That's not a bad idea. It probably wouldn't cost us much more than having several couples for a meal. This way we can have him to ourselves in a way that is certain to be pleasant.

Eating out is not always the solution for two-career entertaining, but it is worth considering. Two-career couples frequently have more money than time and can afford to spend something to make entertaining easier. Even if you decide not to eat out, you can save yourself trouble by employing professional help to entertain at home. At fairly reasonable rates you can hire anything from a full catering service to a high school student who comes in and cleans up afterward.

People who believe that entertaining should be fun are willing to set aside something for it in their budget. A working couple should feel free to use money they earn to buy what they most want in the way of entertainment.

THE NO-CHILDREN PROBLEM

Almost without exception, the people we know without children tell us that they have a special kind of entertainment problem. They have too much time together. We recently asked one thirty-year-old career-woman, "How much time do you spend with your husband?" Her answer: "Too much!" Another working wife, whose husband traveled, said that she liked to have him out of town so that she could get things done around the house.

Couples without children cannot go out every night without growing tired of the same boring round of parties; nor can they stay in every night without getting tired of looking at each other and TV. For these people, planned recreation is especially important for the continuance of a happy marriage. Together they need to work out a reasonable balance between joint and individual recreational activities. Gwynn complains that Abe goes fishing every weekend and leaves her home alone to twiddle her fingers. Evelyn complains with equal vigor that Harry is underfoot all the time and never gets out of the house.

These couples have too much unstructured leisure. They need a dance club or a bridge club. Or, if they're big on organizing, they can start a group that exchanges dinner parties. If they work out this dual activity so that it pleases them both, it will grow naturally to fill all the time they want to give to it. Church activities, volleyball tournaments, and wilderness hikes can become a way of life for those who begin them, sometimes with some degree of hesitation.

In addition to joint activities, each member of the couple needs some interesting separate activity occasionally—such as jogging, tennis, or sailing. Finding ways to spend your spare time is not hard at any age, but it always requires some serious self-evaluation. You need to know clearly what you find gratifying. Political involvement or civic action can be your kind of entertainment. Sometimes controlling a school board can be as much fun as a trip to Aspen. In the next chapter we will discuss civic involvement more fully.

One problem couples without children often face is finding friends who talk about something other than their pregnancies and their children's cute sayings. The conversations at most parties among married couples can bore and irritate the couple without children. The only defense against child-oriented conversations is a satiric monologue about your dog or canary. If you match the doting parent's adulatory tones, you may make him see how boorish it is to talk about something that isn't interesting to everyone in the conversational circle.

But such defensive action does not brighten your social life. You need groups of people who share your interests—intellectual, social, political, recreational—so that more interesting matters replace the child-centered conversation. You may find your closest friends among couples without children, because the gap between parents and nonparents is a wide one.

THE CHILDREN PROBLEM

Couples with children cannot imagine having too much time together. Their problem is the opposite one—too little time. Parents have to accept the fact that their lives are tied up with a permanent multiple grouping. You send your children off to college, and they come home for the summer just when you're about to take a vacation. You get them married, and they spend their vacation with you so that you can watch the grandchildren. As Francis Bacon said, "Children are hostages to fortune."

Since you cannot change this situation, you may as well turn it to your advantage. Unlike childless couples, couples with children never find it difficult to make friends. Children are a strong common bond among families. From the people you meet in the childbirth classes and the doctor's office to the parents at nursery school, PTA, and little league, you will find many who share the dominant interest in your private life—the children. From these people you select the compatible ones and join in a lifelong fellowship of parenthood.

Two-career couples cannot avoid devoting most of their leisure time to the children, but they can at least choose what is most interesting to them about the children and divide their parental duties according to what they most enjoy. You don't have to go to the ballgames, the class programs, the piano recitals, the band concerts, the ballet lessons, and other activities. One of you can take some of them and the other can take the rest. In this case, contrary to the old saying, division is strength.

Of course, since your leisure is limited, you must schedule your time carefully. You can destroy the value of the time you spend with the children if you resent having to participate in their activities. Even small children are extremely sensitive to parental moods. If a parent goes along grudgingly, the child will sense it and is likely to show his awareness with sulkiness or disappointment. You must choose how you want to spend time with your children and then do it gladly.

If you have more than one child, you encounter an almost impossible scheduling problem for recreation. One child always wants to go one direction, and the others want a different one. Your own patience while each is having his turn can teach the children the enjoyment of watching while others have fun. The wife who sits on the bank and watches her husband at his landscape painting may be having as much fun as the painter. She is watching someone she loves get a kick out of his spare time. In the same way, parents can discover—and teach— that giving a delightful experience to someone else is as much fun as fun itself.

EXTENDED VACATIONS

An extended vacation, like other uses of leisure time, should strengthen you physically and emotionally. Unlike other families, though, two-career families may have difficulty finding time when they can both get off together. That in itself is frequently a strain. We have known many working couples who take separate vacations, not because they don't like to be together but because their work requires them to take vacations at different times of the year.

When simultaneous scheduling is impossible, you don't have to feel that the vacation is wasted. You can still benefit from the time if you use it creatively. Admittedly, it might be more fun to take time off together, but vacations are fun with friends as well.

Andy and Helen always had trouble scheduling their vacations. One year Andy's budget was not approved until the end of July. He couldn't leave the office until he had presented it to the board. Helen was regularly scheduled for two weeks in June. As a department store manager, she had to be back before the fall rush began in early August. When it became apparent that they couldn't get away together, Helen blamed Andy and his stupid office system for spoiling the hiking trip they had been planning all winter. They had already made reservations for a Colorado condominium and had purposely not enrolled the two children in swimming lessons so they could go the first two weeks of June.

After the first flurry of disappointment, though, they began to think of alternatives. Helen's college roommate, whom she hadn't seen in years, had children about the same age as Helen's. Helen invited her to bring the children out to share the condominium with her. The result was two weeks of Colorado fun. In August, when Helen was busiest at work, Andy took two weeks at home to panel the basement—a job he had been trying to find time for since they moved in three years before. To his surprise, it was one of the nicest vacations he had ever had because it seemed to be extra time that he hadn't counted on.

Separate vacations for two-career couples are not ideal, but some couples find them better than vacations that are unpleasant for one of them. David and Frances, for example, had good jobs with the same company, she in shipping and he in sales. They had lunch together every day in the cafeteria with their friends at work, drove home together, and worked around the house in the evenings.

They scheduled their vacations together because they assumed that was what married people did. Although Frances never said anything about it, she hated vacation time because she knew what was going to happen. This year, when David began getting his fishing equipment ready a month before their vacation, Frances said quietly, "Don't you think it would be more enjoyable this time to go to the shore where there's more for me to do while you're fishing?"

"Coastal fishing is no fun," David said, rummaging through his tackle box. "We always go to the same place."

"I know," Frances replied, defeat in her tone.

So, for another year, while David got up at dawn and went out along the trout stream, Frances sat in the cabin that didn't have a TV and did needlework that she didn't enjoy. When David came back to the cabin, she helped him clean his catch and then fried the fish, which she did not like, on a two-burner stove that she hated.

Vacations in two-career families are good only if they give both of you pleasure. Frances, as a loving wife, followed where David wanted to go, but it did not benefit her or their marriage. She came home tense and resentful, anxious to get back to work and away from a vacation over which she had no control. If David enjoyed fishing and Frances did not, it would have been better for them to agree on alternating years at the coast and in the mountains.

In this particular two-career family, though, Frances accepted the role of submissive wife. Theirs was a liaison marriage in which she catered to David's desires. She would have been ashamed to admit how resentful she was about vacations because it would not have been appropriate for a wife to make such a decision. David made more money and was therefore the head of the house.

One member of a family ought not to have to endure boredom or discomfort while the other has a good time. The planning that goes into an annual vacation should be shared equally. Keep your options open and don't end up like Frances and David with a vacation that becomes a burden instead of a blessing.

Some couples have such drastically different interests that compromises have to be made. Irv and Sylvia met their disagreement head on. She insisted on going home to visit her parents every summer. He wanted to go to Minnesota to camp. For years they split their two-week vacation down the middle, one week in camp and the other with Sylvia's relatives. Neither of them resented the time spent with the other because they both got to do what they wanted and ended up happy.

A particularly nice kind of vacation is one in which you make money as well as spend it. In addition to the free time you have each year, you can sometimes combine a business trip with time off. If you have to make a field trip or site visit, you may be able to go together. That way you can get in some skiing, fishing, hiking, or sightseeing—even a visit with the relatives—and let the business pay for the pleasure.

Many executives take vacations they don't want and can poorly afford because of social pressures. A quiet vacation at home is better than one that strains the budget and spoils your good humor for six months afterward. The purpose of a vacation is not to impress others but to refresh yourselves.

THE TOTAL PICTURE

According to thinkers like Carl Jung and Josef Pieper, total immersion in something outside your work is revitalizing. You return to work with more creative vigor. Those who only sleep and work grow dull and lose their motivation. Recreation relieves the tedious routine, so that when you get back to work it is no longer dull.

Wise use of leisure time is a matter of proportion, a matter of money, and a matter of taste. You allocate your time off so that you have a chance to do things with your family, with your husband or wife, and, occasionally, by yourself. You don't feel that one of these areas is superior to another. They are all part of a well-balanced recreational program.

But if you are not careful, you may begin to slight one of them. The self-sacrificing person is inclined to give all his time to his family. Typically, he grows resentful when they are not appreciative enough of the sacrifice. Some couples sacrifice for the children. They feel that children should not be left with a babysitter while they take a night out at the movies. They stay home and bicker with the children instead. These choices, though well intended, are going to cause difficulty because they are not made for the right reasons. You have to give yourself some time with each other—and some time for yourself. Then the choice to surrender part of that time for others will not make you feel trapped or defensive about your leisure.

The same holds true of the money you put into recreation. You should allot some of it for the family and some of it for you alone. The person who selfishly stuffs the total leisure time fund into his own equipment collection is not likely to derive anything but disappointment from it. You can hardly expect the family to be glad to see your new golf cart if they have been denied the price of a movie. The best use of funds is for things that will bring pleasure to the whole family.

Taste is a family matter too. Most couples like to do certain things together in their leisure time. Since the parents are the dominant early influences on the children, the children's recreational tastes should grow with those of the parents. This way recreation can become an area of pleasurable participation for everyone. The family freely chooses to romp together through a world that sometimes threatens, but cannot dampen, their joint happiness.

The Joneses Talk About Recreation

Ruth: A good friend of mine told me the other day that she likes nothing better than to take classes at the university. But she has done this only twice in the last ten years. She's deceiving herself about what her values really are in the use of her leisure time.

Bill: You mean that if she really enjoyed going to school she'd do that instead of playing all that bridge? I'm afraid she's telling you the truth, but there's one thing she likes more than learning. She has to have the reinforcing friendship of her bridge club friends.

Ruth: So what we choose for leisure time activities is determined by many desires and needs, not just one simple one.

Bill: Right. She may love and respect learning most of all—in the abstract. But her old friends satisfy a social need that the impersonal classes at the university don't.

Ruth: We're lucky if we're conscious enough of our needs to be able to choose activities that satisfy all of them at once. If we think we're looking for social involvement but *really* need prestige or if we think we're looking for a friend but *really* want the secure world of our childhood, we're bound to be disappointed and unsatisfied in our leisure time.

Bill: And then the descending spiral is activated. We blame the people with whom we share our leisure for the failure of our own dreams, and leisure becomes even less rewarding than before. You've said we should know how to distinguish between the need for social involvement and the need for prestige. Doesn't it take a lot of self-awareness to do that? How do you think busy people get there from where they are now?

Ruth: The simplest way is to ask ourselves why we're doing what we're doing and then try to answer the question as honestly as possible—listening carefully to our answer. I have a friend who is very active in Planned Parenthood. She told me she was attending a national conference because it would be good for her image. She was quite realistic about her reason for going to that meeting.

Bill: I wonder, though, if she meant her self-image or her public image?

Ruth: I think she meant her public image.

Bill: Then she classifies this leisure time activity as part of her public life.

Ruth: She's a real professional. She treats everything, even her recreation, very seriously.

Bill: Then she probably derives the kind of gratification she's looking for from it. I maintain, though, that even if she doesn't admit it, she's glad to get away from her husband and family for a while, glad to be going somewhere to see some interesting people, and glad to have something to talk about for two or three months after she gets home.

No matter how realistic we are about our recreation, it may do far more than we're aware of—either positively or negatively. Your friend seems to have made a wise choice in that her recreation fulfills all her needs, both her conscious needs and her subconscious ones.

Ruth: Yes. But if we're as realistic as we can possibly be in saying why we choose one form of leisure activity rather than another, I think the subconscious needs will take care of themselves.

Bill: You're probably right. Not even your most professional friend is capable of total self-analysis.

8

Civic
Involvement
and
Politics

ALTHOUGH involvement in public affairs is usually a question of personal choice, at times it becomes necessary for professional advancement. At such times it ceases to be a leisure activity and becomes part of your public life. This transitional area between public and private existence often combines professional advancement and private gratification.

Participation in public affairs may involve certain sacrifices, and everyone who has served on a civic committee has been in danger of being bored to death. In spite of the burdens, early in their careers serious professionals probably consider some involvement in civic affairs.

COUPLE TIME

In two-career marriages we should learn to think in terms of couple time when we plan our civic involvement. By keeping in mind the total number of hours that we have together during the week, we will avoid the excessive outside involvement that often causes trouble in a marriage.

Aggie and Errol both had strong political learnings. Before they married, Aggie was active in the local League of Women Voters. The first year of her marriage she was asked to be president of that group. She said she would take the job and was almost immediately asked to become a member of the county Democratic committee, an opportunity she didn't want to pass up. The same year Errol ran for the city council and won the position.

By the second year of their marriage they were going to separate meetings at least four nights a week. Since they had not yet worked out their individual responsibilities around the house, they grew resentful of each other's failure to do more. Aggie ate her large meal at noon in the company cafeteria and settled for a quick sandwich before her evening meetings. Errol had no choice but to fix his own supper. To show his resentment, he left the pans soaking in the sink for Aggie to wash in the morning before work.

Aggie and Errol both believed that their contribution to their community was more important than their home life. They would have had a much happier marriage if they had apportioned their time so that they spent more of it together. As it was, their couple hours dwindled to zero, and their life together was consumed by their civic involvement.

COMMUNITY VISIBILITY

Aggie and Errol both wanted visibility in their community. They had been led to believe that political involvement increases a person's prestige. It may do that; but such visibility can have negative professional consequences as well. Aggie's co-workers resented her political activity and made her as wretched at work as she was at home. They suggested that she was a pushy newcomer who was exploiting her visibility at the expense of her work. Her superiors came to believe that Aggie was letting others do some of her assignments.

We can defend ourselves against such accusations by keeping our superiors informed of the nature and extent of our political involvement. When the boss knows what we are doing in civic affairs and what our motives are, we can counteract the gossip that floats around everyone who becomes visible to the public eye. Only when we rush into positions that we have not checked out with our superiors do we run the chance of professional difficulties.

Civic visibility can also be useful for expanding our social horizons. The people we meet on committees are likely to share our interests and invite us into their circle. Aggie and Errol misused their civic visibility by letting it lead them into separate lives. They spent more time with the people in their civic groups than they did with each other.

We don't have to follow Aggie and Errol's response to civic visibility. By keeping our marriage as the center from which we operate, we can move out as a couple to share the joy of new-found friends who recognize us as civic-minded participants in the world's management.

FAMILY-RELATED CIVIC INVOLVEMENT

The kind of civic involvement we choose frequently grows out of family concerns. Bea and Russ worried, when they moved to Fairmont, that the local school system had no summer programs for their children. The first two summers the children lay around watching TV the way most of their friends did. The third summer Bea decided to do something to change the situation.

She organized a group of concerned parents, and in September they went before the school board to discuss plans for a summer enrichment program for the children. The board's immediate response—we don't have the budget for that kind of program. Bea reported her disappointment to Russ, who discussed the problem with several members of his staff. One of them said, "Why don't you try parks and recreation? They have a big budget."

Russ called around and found out when the parks and recreation board met. He and Bea showed up with some friends at the next meeting, completed proposal in hand.

"We aren't staffed to handle anything that big," the board chairman said. "All we have is a work crew to maintain the parks and playing fields."

"But a lot of the physical education teachers clerk in the summer to make extra money," Russ responded. "Why don't you hire them?"

"We don't have authority to do that," the chairman quickly replied.

Before the evening was over, in spite of the board's resistance, Russ and Bea pushed through the idea of a coordinating committee to work with the school board and the parks and recreation department to develop a summer program for schoolchildren. It took most of the year to develop the program, and the first summer it was far from perfect. But for eleven years now the Fairmont Summer Enrichment Program has been growing. Russ and Bea are still in charge of it, even though both their children are in college.

Like Russ and Bea, you have probably seen plenty of improvements that you would like to make in your environment. Beyond the un-weeded yard and the unpainted garage lies the even more attractive area of civic improvement. It is easy to complain without doing anything, but it can be rewarding to reach out and change your environment for the better.

Personal Concern

Bea and Russ succeeded partly because they began with a deep personal concern for civic improvement. You should not plan to undertake a project unless you firmly believe in it. Halfhearted partici-pation leads only to a self-image of failure—something nobody needs. And you can't be concerned about everything. Bea and Russ were also concerned about their children's math instruction, the lunchroom facilities, and the poor funding the schools received, but they knew that their couple time was limited and that to embark on more than one project would mark them as malcontents and alienate them from the people they had to persuade.

It is better to focus on a single area of improvement and demonstrate by your conversation and actions that you have given this matter considerable thought. In selecting the area of concern, assess your priorities as well as your chances of success. Start with the project you think has the best chance of succeeding. With that first achievement behind you, your second effort will have a better chance. In civic activities success breeds further success.

Confidence

Once Bea and Russ began their campaign for a summer program in the schools, they were confident that they would succeed. Many people doubt that they have any power over civic affairs. But if you look around you at the local level you see that people working for change have a pretty good winning record.

You can sustain the confidence you need better than most people because you are a two-career couple. In your professional lives you are both competing regularly with intelligent people. That competition has warmed you up for the task of working with bureaucrats and politicians who are responsive to voter pressure.

Your most difficult job will be seeking out the true sources of power. Bea and Russ discovered rather quickly that the school board was powerless to make any changes. The board members simply approved the budget that the superintendent submitted and spent the rest of their meeting time bogged down in trivia. The superintendent's office professed its interest in the summer program but passed the responsibility back to the board.

Some reformers would have given up hope in the face of all this red tape in the city system. But Russ and Bea persisted in their belief that they could find the center of power and put pressure on it. Every city system is different, but normally officials with nominal responsibility are not the ones who can bring about a change. You mustn't lose confidence in your efforts until you reach the central power, because finding that responsible authority is half the battle.

Collaboration

Confidence alone is not enough to see you through. Unless you have collaboration, your confidence will flag long before you determine where the power is. To bring about any civic change you have to be able to control a sizable bloc of voters. That means you have to spend a lot of time talking to people in person, telephoning friends of friends, and generally making your presence felt in the community.

Although the collaborators you find will not be as interested in the project as you are, you can move them to achieve your purpose by trading off their interests against your own. Support them in their project, and they will support you in yours. As a manager, you know that this kind of bargaining is necessary if you are going to get anywhere with your project.

Don't let others' apathy spoil your own confidence in your project. Your collaborators mean well, but they may not show up at meetings or may wander off to pursue more immediately attainable goals. By keeping the bright hope of a victory before them, you will gain enough mass support to impress the central powers. That is all you need from your collaborators.

A family-related project such as the one Russ and Bea worked on is the best kind for obtaining support. It benefits many people at relatively little expense. Another popular family-related community project is a tax reduction or tax reallocation program. Nothing unifies a neighborhood more quickly than the prospect of property reassessment or rezoning. When community crises of this sort come along, somebody has to take the lead, and it may as well be you.

Investigation

Even after you find the responsible civic authority and solicit support from other people, you have a lot of investigation to do to make your program succeed. Before you present a big argument, you need statistics on your locality and information on other municipalities with similar programs that are functioning adequately.

You don't have to be a research specialist, but you should get good illustrations from surrounding towns. These will sometimes shame the local authorities into action when nothing else works. Russ and Bea's argument centered on the fact that Fairmont was the only city of its size in the southern part of the state that had no organized summer activities for school-age children.

Other telling arguments include improved quality of living, attraction of more industry, and community prestige. Any of these arguments can sway a city council in your direction. Keep coming back with new data until you draw a positive response from enough civic leaders to win your case.

Persistence

Persistence is essential throughout your efforts, but it is especially important in the last stage of a community project. After you have won a nominal victory and the program has been approved, you sigh with relief and turn to some new interest. Then, after six months, you discover that nothing has been done to implement the change. At this point your persistence must become tenacity. Find out who is responsible for implementing the change and hound them until you see the results you have been working for.

The areas of family-related civic involvement are numerous. For the family with children, school is probably the most promising and rewarding area. Schools change rapidly, and there is always something to improve in nursery school activities, the PTA, or the volunteer aid program. In many of these programs you are not so much concerned with reform or change as with involvement. Funneling your time and energy into existing programs will give you the same rewards as a more drastic change, but with far less effort on your part.

COMMUNITY SERVICE

Beyond family-related civic involvement is the larger area of community service. In every municipality people need help and encouragement. Part of your energy can be devoted to these people. When Steve was thirty-three, he lost his position as regional supervisor of a supermarket chain because of alcoholism. Beth continued to support the family on her salary while Steve went to an alcoholism treatment center.

When he was released from the center, the doctors recommended that Steve move to a new town where he would be free from the influence of his previous social patterns. Beth gave up her job and moved with Steve and the two children to Cobbsville, a town with a population of about seventy thousand. In two years Steve and Beth had good jobs in the same grocery supply center, and the children were happily settled in school.

Beth soon became aware that Cobbsville offered no help for problem drinkers. When one of the men she worked with was hospitalized for alcoholism, the treatment consisted of putting him in a straitjacket and hiring a male attendant to make sure he didn't hurt himself during his withdrawal.

Beth told Steve about the case, and they went to see the man's wife. From this beginning they developed one of the best alcoholism control centers in the state. Steve got funds from the state health department to bring in specialists and, from his study of other such centers, designed a multipurpose organization to aid problem drinkers and their families. After five years, Steve was offered a position as executive director of the state drug and alcohol program. Thus his private concern led him to a new profession.

You too can offer services related to your own experiences or your own needs. A Parents Without Partners chapter, a Big Brother club, and similar service groups are often composed of people whose experiences have made them sympathetic to a particular civic need.

Don't be shy about getting involved. Whatever talents you have can be useful. Older people, minorities, the poor, the handicapped are waiting for someone with spare time. Most communities have a volunteer action center that will evaluate the amount of time and experience you can offer and then put you in a place where your service will be most valuable. And if your community doesn't have such an action center, organize one.

SERVICE CLUBS

A special kind of action group is the service club. You may feel at ease working through an organization such as Kiwanis, Rotary, King's Daughters, or the League of Women Voters. These groups offer regular membership and a regular program of social service. Their education projects, social action programs, and civic improvement campaigns are organized on the assumption that all members will participate as their time and talents permit.

The advantage of these groups is that, unlike community organizations, they have a visible national or international management that is responsive to members' suggestions. Of course, as with all large organizations, change may take time. Still, these clubs can be powerful pressure groups for your projects. And most of the civic leaders in town belong to one or more service organizations.

A civic club gives you visibility for receiving career credit for what you do. Within the group, you develop friendships and areas of influence that are likely to help you advance professionally. Even if the results are not directly apparent, the information you obtain at club meetings will expand your knowledge of the community.

From a personal point of view, the companionship you get through this group can be very satisfying. You share other members' immediate concerns and a conviction that your efforts can bring about positive change. The right service club can give you the confidence and support you need to bring about the social improvement you are seeking.

How do you join a service club? Since membership in most clubs is invitational, you have to make yourself known to the membership committee. That is not difficult, though. You will meet some club members in your professional life. If you let them know that your views correspond with theirs, they will soon have you on the waiting list. Service groups are eager to have new members who want to improve the community. If you are not shy about your interest, you will have no trouble making one of these service teams.

CHURCH SERVICE

Churches are in many ways analogous to service clubs. They can be pressure groups for public service, and they have an existing structure designed for action. Usually, they are more open to new members than service clubs, and their fellowship is frequently as fervent as that of their secular equivalents.

Colin and Vera knew that the church in their hometown provided ready-made action groups for public service. Vera's mother helped serve lunches at the child care center, and Colin's father spent many happy years with the church's literacy action group, teaching adults how to read. When they moved to a new town, Colin and Vera immediately joined a church of the same denomination only to find that it had no civic service groups and didn't want any. When they spoke to the minister about getting the church involved in the community, he told them that they might be happier elsewhere. This church was primarily concerned with saving souls.

Colin and Vera learned the hard way that it is impossible to classify churches by denomination. Churches vary widely in their attitudes toward human need. One can be completely otherworldly, and another with the same denominational ties can be deeply involved in community affairs. An active congregation will give you numerous ways to express your professional and private concerns for civic betterment. Some churches have outreach programs that bring child care to ghettos, retirement facilities to the elderly, and visiting services to hospitals and prisons. And all churches provide social programs for their own members. Nowhere else in town, except perhaps at the country club, can you find so many opportunities for joint family activity. The social activities of a church—from family suppers to annual retreats—give you a chance to meet other people who are interested in civic betterment.

SPECIAL PROJECTS

A quick way to become involved in a civic group is by taking on some of the organization's menial tasks. In many organizations the newcomer is automatically made United Fund chairman for the year. Sometimes he gets his picture in the in-house newspaper. Although his secretary usually handles the actual solicitation and collections, he gets to go to some fund-raising dinners where he meets others in his position. Through his special assignment, he learns the way the organization functions.

The equivalent of this type of assignment in private life is the neighborhood solicitation. In most suburban areas you can live in a community for years and have no reason to go into your neighbors' houses. The special solicitation is the modern version of borrowing a cup of sugar. It puts you in direct contact with the people who live around you.

We had not been in our new neighborhood a month before the March of Dimes chairman called. Would we take our two-block area for the campaign? Before we had finished both sides of the block, we knew the people first hand and second hand. Each family told us first about themselves and then about their neighbors.

Special projects give you an excuse to take time out from your professional assignments and relax on neutral ground. In addition to neighborhood solicitations you may occasionally be asked to participate in a neighborhood improvement project. We were recently offered a chance to participate in our neighborhood protective association. We were to take one night every month to patrol the thirty-house area, scaring off would-be vandals and robbers with our flashlight beam. The project was never implemented, but the sense of community it generated made the neighbors feel as safe as if they were being protected by a civilian patrol. Now they know they are surrounded by well-meaning people with fears and hopes similar to their own.

THE LOCAL POLITICAL SCENE

Two careers are an advantage if you want to participate in local politics, but don't push until you are sure of the sources of power. Local politicians may be jealous of their control and must not feel threatened by your presence. Even though you plan to overthrow them, unless you have a daring offensive ready, you had better step into their territory warily.

The two major ingresses into political activity at the local level are party participation and committee action. Either of these choices can lead to power control. Especially when you work as a husband-wife team, you are likely to move ahead rapidly.

Party Participation

The local party organization is not readily visible. It is usually controlled by a few people who go to meetings that you hardly ever hear about until they're over and some decision has been made. The quickest way to find out who the local party leaders are is to call a city hall official and ask about participation. Elected city officials are quite conscious of what is going on and are glad to have somebody else working for their party.

You can begin by getting involved in preelection activities—making phone calls or handing out leaflets in the neighborhood. A small contribution to someone's campaign can open doors for you too. On election day you serve at the polls or drive people there. Any menial task you do will single you out as a friend of the party. Of course, you'll want to be present at the victory celebration the night of the election because the major candidates will be there.

Then you go to ward meetings, where a dozen or so people come together in a dingy room and determine important matters. Ward officials find candidates for the primaries, take stands on issues, and collect campaign funds. Some neighborhood wards have women's groups, children's groups, young people's groups. They organize everyone who can help collect for the cause. Generally, one or two people determine how the funds are allocated. Disbursement of the funds can be the key to your success in this political area. When you start questioning financial dealings, everyone will treat you with deference.

Although moving up through the party ranks may sound tedious, the work itself is fun and it doesn't take long. When the two of you politick together, you are a team working toward a realistic goal. If you decide to run for an office or seek appointment on some municipal committee, every minute you have put in working for the party will pay off.

Committee Action

Sometimes you can reverse the entrance procedure and begin with a position on a municipal committee. You start by attending city meetings to find out what committees need members. Show some interest at a public meeting, and you will soon be appointed to a committee of your choice.

After their first city council meeting, Lisa and Duane went up to talk to their councilman. They told him they had a special interest in the condition of municipal parks. The one in their neighborhood was so overgrown that gangs of children hid in the underbrush and harassed people so that they were afraid to use it.

The councilman took their names and told them he would see what he could do about the problem. Two days later he phoned them with his report. The parks board had reported the matter to the police several times, but they didn't know what to do. "It's obvious what they should do," Lisa said. "They should clean out the underbrush so the buildings can be seen from the street. That plus a few lights on high poles would discourage the kind of thing that's going on in there now."

Lisa was showing some positive understanding of a problem the politician had not thought about nor cared to think about. This one responded in typical fasion—by offering Lisa a political appointment. "Well," the councilman said, "there's a position vacant on the parks board. Would you like to serve on it?"

Lisa caught her breath and said, "Let me talk to my husband and call you back."

She and Duane decided it would be a good thing to do. Lisa wanted to see how city government functioned. That's why they had gone to the council meeting in the first place. What better way to get involved than by serving on a city board? She called the councilman back and accepted the position. Thus, before she had been in town a year, she was a member of the seven-member governing board of the local parks system.

In her new position she found out about interest groups. She got calls from the playground equipment company, the landscape companies, and disgruntled citizens who had some complaint about the parks. She was so busy that she almost forgot her original complaint—the overgrown condition of the neighborhood park. At the second meeting she mentioned it. "I've thought about this problem a good deal," she told the board. "Parks are going to waste in some areas because good people are afraid to use them. We seem to be trying to make ours as green as possible. That's nice, but when the greenery helps the vandals, we have to cut the greenery." She suggested trimming the trees up eight feet from the ground, clearing all underbrush, and installing night lights.

Although the environmentalist on the board put up some complaint, Lisa got her way. The parks were cleared out and lighted. The project got some attention in the newspaper because it was hailed as a victory for middle-class park users. Children would be safer now, and so would adults.

Lisa was made chairman of the board and became a person of some importance around town. Her activities in this private sector had a salubrious effect on her professional life too. She was elected Woman of the Year for her park work and received a commendation from her employer, who was glad to see company people taking a lead in municipal affairs.

You may feel, as Lisa sometimes did, that you have to put in a lot of dreary committee hours before you see any results. But this is the way improvements are made in a community. The county library board is run by people like you, busy people who wonder if it's worth the effort. But unless people like you make the effort, you will have no programs of old films, a small book budget, and few other services such as children's hours and great books discussions.

Most public agencies work the same way. They are staffed and maintained by well-meaning but overworked professionals. If citizens don't interact with these people, the professionals don't know what is needed. They draw their salaries and wait, while more and more of the budget goes into administrative management and maintenance. Only when interested people get into the committee system do things get done.

Two-career couples can learn the joy of political involvement as a team. Your involvement together can reassure you that you are not helpless creatures. That assurance, and the sense of control that grows along with it, transfers to your work. You learn how to advance professionally by exercising your power in similar situations.

RUNNING FOR OFFICE

If you get deeply enough involved in politics, you may want to run for office. Should you decide on this step, you must talk it over carefully with your family. We know couples who were totally happy together until one of them got involved in a political campaign. Then the troubles began. Campaign tension either brings couples closer together or tears them apart. If you get the wholehearted endorsement of your family before you accept candidacy, you are more likely to make it through with your family intact.

You also need to discuss the situation with your boss to find out how your company feels about political officeholders. Obviously, you can't be a full-time public servant and a full-time employee, but with certain municipal offices such as city council you can manage a career and a political assignment simultaneously. Even if you are running on a nonpartisan ticket, your company may not approve. It doesn't hurt to get an official written endorsement from some high company official before you start campaigning.

Once you have clearance from your family and your company, you still need to think about the endorsement of either your party or some other sizable and visible group. If you are going in for environmental issues, for example, you can get the support of the Sierra Club and the Audubon Society. No one wins an election alone. Group backing gives you psychological support, even if the group has very little to offer you financially.

Visibility during the campaign is essential. If you don't have a number of people in the party working for you, you will have to get friends behind you and make your own campaign headquarters somewhere. Even if the party does endorse you, you still need your own treasurer and secretary to handle the money and the correspondence, You may also need a coordinating manager to call meetings and seek out support.

How much support you get within your profession depends on your career. If your political position will clearly gain credit for the company in the community, your own public relations people may come up with some good ideas. Even if they don't, somebody at work will know the old-time campaigners who can turn out the ethnic vote, the corporate vote, the real estate vote, or other influential blocs.

Newspaper support, too, can get you a lot of votes. A few visits with the local editors will get you some interviews. The interview is one of the secrets of successful campaigning. You have probably watched enough politicians on TV to know that you must be bland but charismatic, rational but emotional, general but profound. In short, you must say nothing with convincing sincerity. But if you are running on a particular issue, you probably will have to come out and make your position clear. Then you win or lose on what you stand for, not your personality.

STANDING UP TO BE COUNTED

Whatever your decision about social and political involvement, keep in mind that you are part of a large American minority—a two-career family. It is easy to become so absorbed in keeping the family together and getting the day's work done that everything else is pushed out of your life. Yet you cannot afford to ignore political affairs entirely. You are paying the taxes and buying the houses—and the breakfast cereal. Your children are the ones in the schools, and your cars are the ones on the roads. When you see something you don't like, speak up and get it changed.

Many two-career couples we have interviewed say without even any great degree of despondency, "We can't do anything about it." But we can. We are the new workers of America—a new managerial class. Although we may not be able to solve the energy crisis or the cancer problem, we can stand up to be counted instead of going down for the count. Here are a few areas where political and social action can make a difference.

Education

The public school system is one of the most responsive to external pressure. It may sometimes take a little negotiating to achieve what you want, but you can usually bring about a change if you persist, as Bea and Russ did with their summer enrichment program.

You don't need to focus on anything as elaborate as a summer program. All you need is a keen critical eye. A mother, calling for her child one day after a girl scout meeting, saw another child crying because the school office was closed and there was no phone available for the child to call her mother. The girl didn't know what to do. After the woman had taken the girl home, she called the school principal. "You need a phone in the hall when the school office is closed," she told him.

He thought at first that she was simply a pest who would go away, so he told her he would see about it. In a month she called back to find out why the phone hadn't been installed. He didn't have the funds, there wasn't any place to put it, and he hadn't had a chance to get in touch with the phone company. "Then I'll take care of it," the woman said. "I'll talk to the city superintendent."

"Never mind," the principal said, defeated. "I'll take care of the phone."

Two days later the woman was over to see about the phone. It was plugged in outside the principal's office. Students use it all the time when their parents forget to pick them up or when they have unexpected business late at school. The principal bragged at a principals' meeting about his new phone, and now phones have been installed in all the elementary schools in the community.

Sometimes parents seek more drastic educational change. Personnel matters and curriculum matters are both delicate areas, but both can give way under parental influence. One sour-minded teacher was transferred from the first grade to the upper grades because discontented parents opposed her influence on their young children. And in one high school a more realistic science program was instituted as a result of parental lobbying.

The Arts
In education, of course, people can work through established parents' organizations as well as through the structure of the educational system. No such pattern exists for raising a community's cultural level. Still, the artistic consciousness of a community can be transformed by people with the confidence and the conviction that they can bring about a change.

Jay and Clara had played in the orchestra in college. Their children were interested in studying violin and cello. Since the local schools had no strings program, they found private teachers for their children. After several years of instruction, the children were ready to perform. "Why isn't there a youth orchestra in town?" Jay asked.

"Obviously because nobody has ever organized one," Clara replied. And Jay knew what they were in for. Now, ten years later, the town has an orchestra and a strings program in the public schools. Jay and Clara are playing string quartets with their children and others who have benefited from the program.

Recreation

Managerial leadership can also get you a bowling league or a softball team. We have seen a community that had only a few poorly maintained tennis courts transform itself in a frenzy of tennis fever. From a time when two lonely people lobbed the ball across a dangling net, people are now talking about their game as if they were preparing for Wimbledon. What did it take? A few people who care enough to invest their spare time in organizing tournaments and lessons.

Cooperatives

The idea of social cooperatives is especially attractive to energetic two-career couples. You both believe in positive action for a particular cause. And you are realistic enough to choose a cause that can be achieved. With a few other families you can develop cooperative organizations from which a large number of people will benefit.

Country clubs are an example of thoroughly respectable social cooperatives. Families band together, to start with, and build themselves a place for private recreation, usually around a golf course. Cooperative clubs can be formed around any activity, from tennis to ice skating. By advertising for membership and setting up a board, you form a neighborhood swim club, with an Olympic-size pool that will provide lessons and pleasure for the whole family.

One couple began a small health food business that developed into a community co-op. They started by ordering their nonhomogenized peanut butter from a bulk warehouse and selling off the rest. Then they did the same with their whole-grain wheat. Gradually the business expanded until they had to get a building to house their products. They sold memberships and hired a purchasing agent who managed the co-op for them.

There are endless possibilities for social change and political action. We are not helpless pawns in the hands of an invisible power. We have the power to effect change, beginning at the local level. And our sense of free choice gives us the vision to see what needs changing.

The Joneses Talk About Civic Involvement

Bill: I wonder if people with two careers and a family really have time for civic involvement.

Ruth: You have just described a group that is by definition involved. Their careers and their children put them into the community, whether they like it or not. It's just a question of what kind of involvement they want—active or passive.

Bill: I see your point. Since they pay taxes, have children in public schools, drive on public roads, they're part of the civic scene. If they want to be controlled by others, they can be. But the aggressive role will be taken by someone, and if they give it over they may suffer because of their inactivity.

Ruth: Each family has to choose the area in which it wants to be active. No family has the time to be active everywhere. Overextension simply brings dissatisfaction and wasted effort.

Bill: How do you suggest a family go about choosing the area for its civic involvement?

Ruth: It seems the family's own interests would determine that. If they don't immediately find the opportunity they want, they can choose a related area and move toward their central concern.

Bill: What do you think is the greatest hindrance to satisfactory public involvement for two-career families?

Ruth: Lack of time—especially if there are children, although some activities with children could include community involvement. Some people find the most effective way of becoming involved is through their own professional specialty.

Bill: You're right. We've never run for political office, but you and I have both made so many speeches around town that everybody in political office knows what we think on most subjects. Each person has to consider not only his interest but his ability as well. I'm too impatient with municipal red tape to take the public office route, but

I'm perfectly willing to contribute money and time to someone else's campaign. And I'm not averse to giving my successful candidate advice after he's taken office.

Ruth: Civic involvement is more than just a way of contributing to the community. It can also bring personal reward—such as expanded horizons for one's talents, personal contacts, and avenues for professional change or advancement.

Bill: It's easy to settle for the clichés that work sometimes in politics. But I do think that it is better to act than to sit, better to work than to gripe.

Ruth: Since you feel that way, let's move on to the next chapter.

9

Postmarital Education

EDUCATION is often an area of intense unconscious competition in two-career families. Our self-worth is derived to a large extent from how much we have—financially and intellectually. The lower-paid member of a two-career family often defends himself by asserting his intellectual superiority. When the wife is not a wage earner, she sometimes develops a condescending attitude toward her husband. "He's a good provider," she says, "but he hasn't had time to learn about the finer things of life." By "finer things" she means the things she knows.

Whether they are competing with each other or simply seeking an opportunity to grow, more and more adult Americans are taking advantage of programs in continuing education. Female students over thirty are now the most rapidly increasing educational group in the country.

Adult education is a permanent part of our culture. We are no longer confusing "education" with school attendance. We see that structured study programs are the most efficient route to professional advancement and personal growth. With our training in good management techniques, we look for those agencies that can teach us what we don't know and want to know.

As with friendship and civic involvement, we must balance the time we put into our continuing education program against the other demands of our career and marriage. Our couple hours can be quickly consumed by the demands made on us by an adult education course.

Education is valuable in any family—unless it is used as an excuse to avoid the painful but necessary adjustments of married life. Ike and Annette, for example, got married while Ike was still in school. Annette supported him with her salary and did most of the housework so that Ike could devote his time to finishing his degree. When Ike took a job, Annette expected him to spend more time helping her around the house, since she was still working too.

Ike, though, was not comfortable with housework or with Annette. He preferred his associations at school. The result was that he got three master's degrees while Annette continued to work at sending him to school. Each time he finished, he would say, "Now we can settle down to a normal married life." But within a semester or two Ike would be back in a course that he thought would make him more marketable.

There are numerous reasons for wanting more education, but couples should be sure that they agree on their educational purposes. People can enrich their lives with adult education experiences, but they can also deplete them by unwise involvement. This chapter will help you evaluate continuing education in the context of a two-career marriage so that you can make the best choices among the possibilities available to you.

PEER PRESSURE

Even if we are not nudged back into the classroom by competition within the family, the pressure from those around us often drives us there. Such motivation is not harmful, but we should be sure it is pressing us in the right direction. Alice was in charge of the shipping department of an electrical equipment company. During her five years with the company, she noticed that people often got promoted after they went off for summer conferences. She talked to her husband, Greg, who said he would use his vacation time to take care of the children if she really wanted to enroll in a conference.

Her boss was not as encouraging as her husband. He told her that the company would send her, but he also told her that he didn't think a summer conference would be useful in her particular position. "Then what would be?" she countered. "Others have been promoted as a result of going to conferences."

The boss put her in for the conference, and she went away for three weeks to a training center near San Francisco. From the beginning, Alice's attitude was poor. She thought she knew more about actual working conditions than the theorists who were teaching the sessions. To her, the course was only a compilation of truisms derived from daily management experience.

The report came back to the company that Alice was not a satisfactory participant. Alice gave the conference an equally unsatisfactory evaluation. Greg had wasted his vacation and expected gratitude from Alice, who was too disgruntled to give it to him.

Alice should have waited until she found something she really wanted to learn. Instead, she rushed into a meaningless educational activity that wasted time and spoiled her attitude for constructive learning. What her boss knew, and she didn't, was that managerial training is by necessity extremely specialized, and what may be valuable theoretical training for one person is lost on another.

Peer pressure can work the opposite way too, as it did for Alice's husband Greg. Several of the older men Greg worked with were thoroughly disenchanted with continuing education. "We know more than the people who run those courses," they said. "Why should we sign up for one of them? We know all we need to know for this job." So Greg let several interesting short courses go by. These courses might have given him a chance to discuss his professional situation with people outside his immediate job situation, but the know-it-alls at work were not interested in having him expand his understanding beyond their control.

Thus, as well as being pressured into useless educational experiences, we can be pressured out of valuable opportunities. Our peers may have developed an antieducational attitude that makes it dangerous to reveal any interest in learning or advancement. That closeminded pressure is more difficult to handle than the other because it is so insidious. We have a full-time job that we understand. What else do we need? The answer is nothing if we want to stay where we are forever.

Educators know that they can't teach anybody something if he thinks he knows everything already. Greg's colleagues had that mind set. They scoffed at organizational offers for time off to attend a computer seminar. "We've been running the computer longer than the guys teaching the course. We know its capacity." When the copies of the in-house newsletter came around, they jokingly tossed it into their wastebaskets. "File thirteen," they shouted, "with the rest of the garbage." They prided themselves on their wit, which, like their educations, had fossilized years before.

Those around us tend to determine our attitudes. Education, rightly used, frees us from the slavery of peer domination. Greg and Alice would have been better off with appropriate continuing education, but they let their peers determine their lives for them. We break free of peer pressure by developing the confidence to make our own educational choices.

Knowing You Don't Know

Without debasing ourselves or our present position, we can determine where our present knowledge is deficient. Peer comparison helps in this evaluation. Look at those who are making it, and ask yourself what they know that you don't know. Alice's trouble was in assuming that a conference carried some magical quality that would automatically gain her advancement. She would have done better to ask what those who had advanced knew.

In this evaluation process, two careers are an advantage. You have two professional points of view from which to work. Your double professional vision gives you a deeper perception. By talking to each other about your educational needs—professionally and privately—you can reach a better understanding of what you need to know.

Knowing How to Know

Although humility is a prerequisite for learning, it must not darken into despair. Once you find out what you don't know, you must discover how to learn it.

Ellen worked as a research librarian in a large hospital library. She had a master's degree in library science. When she took the job, she was assigned a staff of eight shelvers, three bibliographers, three secretaries, and four file clerks. Since her experience had been in a small academic community, the new situation intimidated her. Within a few months staff morale deteriorated to the point where shouting matches were followed by sulking silence. Ellen told her husband John that she was going to quit. "I'm a failure," she said in tears. "I don't know anything about personnel management, so what good is all my library science going to do me?"

John, who was supervisor of the claims division of a large insurance company, felt sorry for Ellen, but he couldn't understand her problem. "There's nothing to it," he said. "Just tell them what to do, and see that they do it."

"It's not that simple," Ellen said. "You learned how to handle people as you advanced in your business. I've never seen the way it's done in libraries or anywhere else."

"You learned library science," John said. "You can learn personnel management the same way. Our company is running management courses all the time. I never had much use for them, but you better get yourself into one of them."

Ellen did not have to go to John's company to take the management course. Her hospital offered one quarterly as part of its intern training program. She signed up for it and took it along with the new MDs. Although they talked in terms of nurses, nurses' aides, and budgets, Ellen translated the information to suit her situation.

By the end of the first year Ellen had spotted the troublemakers on her staff and had talks with them. Before long the mood changed, and the doctors who used the library commended Ellen on the quiet, efficient service they found there. "I'm glad you knew about management training," Ellen told John. "I didn't know such a thing existed."

Ellen and John's double vision helped Ellen out of her despair and into the right educational situation. She could have taken another dozen library science courses without accomplishing what one short course in personnel management achieved. She got some good advice on what she needed to know and found out where to learn it.

Knowing Why

We are not always alert to our educational needs. Sometimes we don't know why we need to learn something until we've started learning it. Often our initial motivation is quite low.

Max was a successful sales manager for an athletic supply house. He supervised seventeen regional distributors and he had been doing a good job for seven years. One day his boss called him in and suggested that he take a course in public speaking. Max was taken aback. He was overworked already, and he had just gone through an annual sales conference that had left him exhausted. "Why would I need a course in public speaking?" he asked in as controlled a tone as he could muster.

"You're good with your sales personnel individually," the boss said, "but your public presentations are sometimes weak."

Max enrolled for the night course offered in the management training program. When he arrived the first night, he discovered that he was ten years older than the rest of the students. His face flamed red, and he clenched his teeth while he tried to listen to the instructor. "What am I doing here?" he thought. "This is insulting and debasing. I do my job well. I shouldn't have this inflicted on me."

When he got up to make his first speech, he was so self-conscious that he couldn't get through without reading from his notes. In his private conference afterward he told the instructor he had no need to speak better but that his boss had forced him to take the course. "Your boss is right," the instructor said. "Your self-consciousness and your dependence on notes suggest professional insecurity. A few experiences in this class will give you more assurance."

Max came through what he continued to see as a humiliating experience with more confidence than before. He was happier in his work than he had been for seven years, and before long he had a higher-paid position in public relations, an advancement his boss had expected once Max learned to work with less tension and antagonism.

We may not always know why we need to go through an educational experience, but sometimes our organization will shove us in the right direction even when we are dragging our feet. It is better, of course, to discover our educational shortcomings ourselves—through talks with our superiors or with friends—and then undertake the right kind of learning experience.

EDUCATIONAL PURPOSES

Confused purpose sometimes causes two-career couples to disagree about the why of knowing. When we started school as children, we had no choice about education. Later, we continued for a number of reasons—other people we knew were still going, we thought it would help us get ahead, school was better than any alternative we could think of at the moment. The learning process that continues into our professional life has many purposes too. We encounter trouble in our private lives when one partner does not respect the other's educational aim.

Tom spent $200 on scuba-diving equipment and paid $185 for a course. Jane was so irritated by her husband's extravagance that she bought an $800 sewing machine with free lessons included. Tom's scuba equipment is now piled in the basement because he didn't finish the course. Jane has not yet learned how to use her buttonhole attachment because she didn't get around to starting the free lessons. Tom was not buying an education but trying to make a Caribbean dream come true with his purchase. Jane was only trying to get back at Tom. Jane and Tom should have examined their real purposes and discussed them together before they invested in each of their "educational" programs.

Scuba diving and sewing are not unworthy skills, but they have to be undertaken for realistic, positive reasons. Here are the educational purposes most commonly expressed by career-oriented couples, who are beginning to realize that life is an intricate combination of work and pleasure.

Professional Advancement

Getting ahead is the strongest educational motivation for people between the ages of twenty and forty. Sometimes they enroll in graduate school or professional schools. More often, they take training courses to improve their skills. In companies that stress in-house training, their motivation often arises from peer pressure or from superiors. Whatever the source of the pressure, though, the purpose is still to advance professionally.

Getting ahead is a natural desire, but it is not without its drawbacks. As we have seen earlier in the chapter, undirected technical training can lead to bitterness or jealousy. Sometimes desperation is at the root of professional advancement. Someone who is in a dead-end position or who has limited abilities in his particular job puts his faith in short courses or technical training schools.

No matter how many courses you take, if you are not suited for your job or if the courses are inappropriate for your advancement, you are wasting time and money. When you are inspired to get ahead, find out first what it takes. Talk to people who have made it and listen to them rather than to those who encourage you because they want to get you off their backs or out of their office.

Chet was the junior partner of a law firm that handled the legal affairs of three large trucking companies. Over and over Chet found that his inexperience in trucking terminology was a handicap. He took a leave one summer and enrolled in Northwestern University's School of Transportation. There he learned things he needed to know. Two years later one of the trucking firms hired him as its full-time labor negotiator, a special position with a big future.

Whether someone else points you the way in a professional education or whether you find it yourself, you have to keep your purpose clear. You are getting the training because you want to advance. If it is not relevant to your needs or if you already know what's being taught, there's no point putting in more time and money. Look somewhere else for the training you need to get ahead.

Personal Interest

As we develop professionally, we also reach out for new skills to supplement our private lives. Lessons in weaving, pottery making, and swimming are as popular in continuing education programs as public speaking and personnel management. Many of these skills, of course, are only tangentially related to work. Office-bound people need some tension-relieving activity to help them stay in condition so that they can do a good day's work. Whether the new interest is physical exercise or intellectual involvement, it will contribute to our longevity.

When we begin to wonder if life is nothing but the daily grind, we suddenly find that we are excited about something totally unexpected—anything from rose culture to the Civil War—and we search out people who know more about our new interest so that we can learn from them. Other people, though, still working on the computer short course, find us hopelessly flippant if we tell them about the First Battle of Bull Run or our Mr. Lincoln roses.

We must make an effort to keep our special interest under control. Carson was beginning to stagnate at his job, so he decided what he needed was an outside interest. He talked to someone who suggested that he take a night course in acting. His friend made the suggestion at cocktails one afternoon, adding half in jest, "You've always been a flamboyant personality who enjoyed showing off."

The next week Carson reported to his friend that he had enrolled. "It's what I've always wanted to do," he said. "I can't thank you enough for that suggestion. They're having tryouts for *Oklahoma* next week, and I'm pretty sure to get the part of Judd."

Carson went on from one dramatic success to another, but he gave his job less and less attention. He would drag in after a late performance and sit glassy-eyed at his desk, even after three cups of coffee. He became a night person, with the habits and the pleasures of the theater replacing those of his professional life.

Before he finished his advanced acting course, he had lost his wife as well as his job. "I don't care," he said. "I'm going to New York and try to make it on Broadway." When his friend who had first suggested the acting course last heard from him, he was driving a truck during the day in some of the least desirable sections of town and performing at night in even less desirable ones.

We can sometimes use our educational opportunities to move off in new directions, but we should not let our leisure time educational interest replace job or marriage. Nor should we assume, as Carson did, that a few quick courses will qualify us for a new career. We should be realistic in our appraisal of the opportunities in other areas before we reject what we now have.

Community of Concern

Sometimes our primary educational aim is to find a group of people who are interested in the same areas we are. This community of concern can motivate either professional training or personal interest. We often believe that we are the only person in the world with a certain need. A classroom experience or a conference sometimes gives us a sense of the larger, concerned community.

Catherine was the managing editor of an academic press where she supervised ten copyeditors who prepared manuscripts for publication. As she told her husband Cary, her major problem was antagonism among the proofreaders. Sometimes three of them would not be speaking to each other so that coordinating proofs was difficult.

"Why don't you talk to people at other presses when you're at the convention and see what they do about such situations?" he suggested.

But the conversations at the convention were all the same. Human relationships were a major problem among proofreaders. Since two people had to read the manuscript to each other to check for errors in the printed proof, tension usually developed when one of them made too many mistakes. "Well," Catherine said at the end of the convention, "if nobody knows any more than I do, we're in a pretty bad fix in the publishing business."

Back in the office she saw a notice in *Publishers Weekly* for a three-day training session in office procedures. "I'm a fool to fall for the advertisement," she told Cary, "but I think I'm going to sign up for this training session. It may give me some ideas. I'm desperate."

As she suspected, much of the session was a repetition of the obvious, but the people attending were given a chance to talk about their problems. Under the leader's guidance, they discussed Catherine's proofing problems. "We've been through all that," one of the participants said. "We use tape cassettes."

"What do you mean?" Catherine asked.

"Instead of having two people read to each other, we have one person read onto a tape cassette and then have the other person listen to the tape. That way we have a permanent record of the manuscript and can go back over it as many times as we need to."

Catherine took the idea home with her and found that she saved time and improved office morale simultaneously. The proofreaders' morale rose because they were now working independently and could enjoy each other without feeling threatened. The training session demonstrated to Catherine that she was part of a larger community of concern.

Direction Finding

At some point in our careers we may begin to feel a lost sense of purpose. In these times of professional doubt, some educational experience can help us find a reasonable direction again. If we are not impetuous, we can usually discover some direction to take without any drastic professional disruption.

Sam is an example of someone who made a successful direction change. He was supervisor of the drafting department for the state highway department, but he hated indoor work. When he started as a civil engineer he had worked outdoors, but now all he did was sit at a desk and write memos. His job dissatisfaction made him sullen and unhappy at home as well as at work. His wife Mia was an elementary school principal who enjoyed what she did. She could not understand why Sam didn't enjoy working with the draftsmen. "You've got as large a budget and as many people to supervise as I have," she told him. "Relax and enjoy it."

But their personalities were different. Mia liked supervisory work. Details and memos were part of the daily routine she enjoyed. Sam wanted more freedom from close contact with other people. "Why don't you start looking around for something else to do," Mia suggested. "You're not married to that job."

Sam found that a university in his area offered night courses, and he looked through the offerings to see what was available. The course description that interested him most was one entitled "Environmental Management." Environmentalism was a new field that had opened up since Sam's graduation; he knew nothing about it. At the end of the course he was so excited that he asked for a six-month leave and took a full semester of environmental engineering. At the end of the semester one of his professors suggested that the highway department should assign someone responsibility for environmental surveys.

Sam wrote up a proposal for his department and was given a new assignment. Now he travels around the state talking to people in areas where new highway programs are being planned. He studies the topography and tries to anticipate shifts in wildlife patterns, real estate values, and other environmental changes that a highway could make. He has no one to supervise, and he and Mia are making more money than before.

To find a new direction for ourselves, we must be like Sam. We have to admit that we are now headed in the wrong one. Then we have to take positive steps to educate ourselves in an area that we find interesting. If we are just generally dissatisfied with ourselves, we will never find the right direction. We have to make a positive educational commitment to change.

Expanded Living

Many people take adult education courses simply to enlarge their lives. At all stages of our careers a zest for living comes from an assurance that more interesting things always remain to be learned in life. This awareness of plenty keeps us motivated and alert.

Muriel and Harold are a wretched couple. Their immense world-weariness grows out of their conviction that they know everything. Without even being asked, Muriel tells casual acquaintances, "Harold has read everything in his field. There's nothing left for him to learn about it." And when someone asks them if they subscribe to *The Wall Street Journal*, they reply, "It's the same old thing over and over. Why go on reading it?" Educational apathy as deep as this cannot be motivated. Muriel and Harold are shriveling intellectually, convinced of their superiority. The perpetually young mind is the flexible one, like Sam's, always searching for knowledge with faith that a new world is waiting to be discovered.

SOURCES OF EDUCATIONAL ADVANCEMENT

As long as we are alive, we are learning. Much of our learning is an unconscious accumulation of detail in areas we already know. Yesterday we didn't know the prime interest rate for today; now we do. Last year we thought Mars might sustain life; now we don't think so.

These pieces of information come to us helter-skelter from the media and from conversations. Such unstructured learning is a normal part of living. Occasionally, though, we seek more formal sources of education to gain knowledge that will benefit us in our home life or our career. Here are some of the most common sources of educational advancement.

The Academic Way

"I didn't know anything about changing washers," Vernon said, "so I went to the library and checked out a book on it." If you have been brought up in a reading environment, you probably turn to books to learn what you don't know. If you are trying to find the best make of vacuum cleaner or the most efficient car, you go to the library and check out a book that will tell you the results of current marketing research. If you want to know about tax law, you read another book.

This academic approach is fine as long as you are interested in established, generally accepted knowledge. Colleges and books are repositories for what is already widely known. They tend to be conservative about new areas of learning—the so-called frontiers of knowledge. Classifications, facts, processes now in use—these are the things you can find out from the academics. If you want to learn about

new methods of doing things or discover new, creative ideas, you may
need to look for a different educational source.

Technical Schools

Like universities, technical schools specialize in generally accepted
knowledge. They are not places for experimentation, but what they
teach is clearly designed to contribute to skill in a particular area.
University schools of business offer technical training, as do most
specialized industrial schools.

Claire went directly from high school into marriage and an office job
as a cashier. She began to realize that she was going to have the same
job for the rest of her life unless she took some action to change the
situation. Since she needed to work, full-time college was out of the
question. In any case, she didn't think that academic courses would
help her professionally. She decided to look into various schools of
business.

The one she found offered night courses in banking procedure,
personnel management, computer science, statistics—things that
Claire's bosses knew. She designed a program that covered the topics
she heard about at work. Within three years she was given a branch
office to manage, one of the first women in the city to get such a job.
Claire overcame her educational handicap by suiting her adult education to her professional needs.

Reputable technical schools are closely allied to the businesses for
which they prepare people. Some schools, though, have very ques-
tionable accreditation. During the 1950s and 1960s the flood of GI
benefit money led to the creation of "extension schools" that were
designed to get a maximum of funds for a minimum of instruction.
Many of these are still around. Some of them advertise on TV and in
trade journals. The only way to determine if the school you choose is
reputable is to check its standing with your profession and to make sure
you're getting what you pay for if you enroll.

Short Courses

For most professional people the most efficient kind of education is
on-the-job training designed for their needs. Large companies often
contract for this education in the form of refresher courses or short-
term courses to be taken at nights or on the weekend.

Large companies offer a variety of short courses rather frequently.

Boeing Aircraft, for example, has full-time education officers at most of its plants. These people work with staff members to make sure the courses needed for job improvement are provided at convenient times. Smaller companies often have a relatively limited curriculum.

Short courses are also offered at most community colleges and regional extension divisions. If your company doesn't have a program, look around for catalogs from the schools in your area. You can then plan your own educational future.

Conferences

Even more specialized than short courses are conferences and seminars on a specific problem or topic. People of different backgrounds who share an interest in a subject meet to study it together. Original thinking and valuable learning often result because the occasion is so finely focused and the subject so narrow.

Although some annual professional conferences can be rather dull, you should be able to find a panel or a section where something exciting is taking place. Sharing your thoughts with others in your profession can send you back to work with renewed interest and insight. You don't have to wait for someone else to plan conferences for you. You can make your own to suit your needs. Suppose you are worried about the impact of new federal legislation on your profession. You find a specialist from industry, bring in a governmental official, and invite some people from around the country to join you while you interact with the panel you have designed.

Of all the sources of learning, this one is probably the most flexible and the most immediately rewarding. You don't have to make it a national conference, either. You can hold an office conference for the same purpose, with people from several sections participating. You are probably so accustomed to office conferences that you hardly recognize them as educational experiences. Yet, when you finish talking together, you have always learned something. Even if you haven't found out anything new, you know how people think on a subject—and that may be the most important thing an education can do for you.

THE COMMUNITY OF LEARNING

People who believe in learning have an optimistic drive that others lack. Despair and apathy come from ignorance, and learning can save you from that. When you think you've come to a bad spot either in your marriage or in your job, look around for what you might learn to get you out of the difficulty.

You will retain your faith in education longer if you are discriminating about what you learn. Undifferentiated learning can be disappointing. One Washington executive took courses in Russian, landscape painting, and investment policy three nights a week. One afternoon a week he devoted to his golf lesson. He was also taking piano and studying transcendental meditation. This program was less an education than an escape from life.

To gain from our educational experiences, we have to be willing to make an effort. A psychologist conducted an experiment at a men's club. He sent in one of his students who told the men about an exercise program they could do at home. He offered them free brochures explaining exactly how to do it. Three men stopped by afterward to pick up the brochures.

Two months later the psychologist sent in another student who offered to sell the men a $20 exercise spring that would solve all their physical ailments. Twenty-two of the club members bought one.

The point the psychologist made was that we are willing to spend our money but not to invest our time. People often enroll in adult education courses without considering the investment of time that is required. They attend a session or two and then drop out. It is better not to get started than to start and quit. If you need continuing education, you should get it, but make sure your purpose is clear and your schedule reasonable. Otherwise, you may lose your faith in learning and your joy in living.

The Joneses Talk About Education

Bill: Many of my students are so disillusioned that they don't hesitate to tell me that education does more harm than good. What do you think of that attitude?

Ruth: I wonder what harm they're referring to.

Bill: I think they mean harm to the educated person himself—that the process destroys the spontaneous response to living. I must admit, looking at some of the educated people they've taken courses from, that a Ph.D. is not an automatic promotion to "perfect creature."

Ruth: Nobody but a Ph.D. ever thought it was. The idea of the noble savage is a very attractive one. If goodness and nobility come naturally, one is spared the pains of education. Most education is aimed at cultivating skills and inculcating knowledge. These do not necessarily lead to virtue.

Bill: No, but I still believe that the person who has cultivated his natural potential through an appropriate education is more likely to be free of tension and agreeable than one who has not had continuous intellectual and physical development.

Ruth: I agree. I think our discussion in this chapter emphasized the professional and practical results of an education rather than its personal and psychological value.

Bill: That's frequently the emphasis in education, but I think we all want happiness as much as anything else, and I don't believe we're attributing too much responsibility to education if we say that it's one good way to achieve it. Just because some educated people are offensive, we ought not to discredit education as a means of personal as well as professional improvement. As we are wont to say, "If you think they're bad now, think what they would be without an education."

Ruth: What do you think about having a job or profession that is not at all related to your educational background and interests? Won't this produce a great deal of tension? What about the Harvard-educated stockbroker we know who reads Greek for an hour every morning before he goes to work?

Bill: I think he's a healthy example of how learning can expand life. He's both a stockbroker and a Greek scholar. He has merged the two nicely, and each of these interests keeps him from the narrow-minded belief that there is only one useful activity in the world. Then there is Wallace Stevens, a great poet and a successful insurance agent simultaneously. It's more the attitude than the education that determines whether it harms us or not. If a study of the arts leads to a scorn of practical business pursuits, then we've been miseducated. But if the arts teach us to respect the fullness of life, then they are the enrichment they ought to be.

10

Two-Career
Money
Management

FEW of us would work at the jobs
we have unless we were making money. Since economic necessity is
usually a major motive for professional activity, the way we manage it
influences every area of our marriage. If we don't agree on family fiscal
policy, the resulting tensions create resentment and quarreling.
Money and sex are so intricately related psychologically that even our
sexual relationship can be harmed by squabbles over money.

Money, in small or large amounts, represents purchasing power. In
healthy two-career marriages this power is shared. Frank monetary
conferences precede major purchases so that both partners take responsibility for them. In less satisfactory marriages, one member of the
family is either hopelessly prodigal or hopelessly stingy. When such
differences exist, a good deal of love and understanding are necessary
to work out a reasonable financial plan. Sound money management

involves recognition of the pressures that develop around money. And after we identify those pressures we must find ways to relieve them.

In our society, money represents more than buying power; it also gives people a sense of self-worth. We measure our success by our salaries or by the size of the budgets we control. Here is one example.

Ancil and Deanna were friends with Lee and Joyce. Each couple's combined income was about $35,000. All four enjoyed the same kinds of entertainment. They camped together on weekends and played cards together once or twice a month. They occasionally discussed financial matters, but their relationship was largely a social one.

After several years Lee moved to a position that required him to administer an $8 million budget. Although his salary remained approximately the same as Ancil's, his daily professional activity was now more directly related to financial matters.

As a result of this professional change, the two couples' private relationship deteriorated. Ancil said that Lee had grown snobbish and distant. Lee told Joyce that Ancil and Deanna were dull and common. Before long they were looking for new friends. Thus money management can work strange changes, even when the money isn't ours.

WHOSE MONEY?

In lovenest marriages the passive member of the couple gratefully accepts what the other one hands out, even though both may be working. In this traditional male-female division of responsibilities, the husband enjoys demonstrating his prestige by buying elegant clothes and jewels for his wife—or a washing machine and a crock pot. The wife is the recipient of largesse rather than the co-manager of the purse, and she defers to her husband's opinion in financial matters. Even in the most enlightened marriages, remnants of these traditional patterns sometimes pervade people's thinking. Here are three couples whose different attitudes toward money mark them as antagonists, parellelists, and uniteds.

The Antagonists

Don and Melissa agreed to have a two-career marriage, but they were unable to carry the partnership through because of their previous training in husband-wife roles. Don was in a two-year management training program for an oil company, and Melissa was assistant manager of the cosmetics department in a large department store. Melissa was making more than Don while he was in the program, but Don was scheduled to receive a sizable salary increase when he completed his training.

Melissa was apprehensive about money and reluctant to spend it. Don felt that they should buy a house immediately and begin living well instead of biding their time in a rented place. Melissa agreed, with the understanding that they manage on what furniture they had until Don finished his training. "Oh, all right," Don said, "but it doesn't hurt to look. I enjoy shopping for furniture."

So did Melissa. They enjoyed going around to furniture stores on the weekends, but they often ended up arguing when they got home because Don had seen a bargain that he didn't want to pass up.

One day Melissa came home to find Don sitting happily on a yellow velvet sofa. "I just couldn't resist," Don said. "It was such a bargain that I bought it for you."

Melissa exploded. "How can you make a major investment for my living room without even consulting me—and after you promised to wait!"

"Why do you always have to take the fun out of everything?" Don replied. And the battle was on.

Clearly, Melissa, with her superior income and somewhat conservative marriage-role orientation, felt that she had a double right to decide what went into *her* living room. Don, on the other hand, was exercising the masculine prerogative of buying presents for his wife, even though it was her money that he was spending and even though they had agreed not to use it in that way.

When the smoke cleared, Don promised not to do it again and Melissa forgave him. But Don couldn't forget the insult to his masculinity. At Christmas, when Melissa bought him three shirts and two ties, he remarked, "How can you select what I should wear if I can't have the privilege of selecting what we're both going to sit on?" And they were off again.

Before Don's training program was over, the only money they were glad to spend was the lawyer's fee for the divorce. They didn't argue over that. Their marriage collapsed because Don still wanted a lovenest relationship even though Melissa was making the major share of their income.

Melissa and Don were smart young people but they did not recognize the emotional power of money. From the beginning of their marriage they failed to view it realistically. Consequently, money became the focal point of their antagonism. Don didn't want to admit that he was dependent on Melissa's salary and used his credit buying to create an illusion of wealth. Melissa was afraid of poverty and slightly possessive about her own salary. If their marriage had been more firmly based on a realistic partnership, where the choices were made through continuous consultation, they could have worked out a compromise to help them survive their two years of deprivation.

The Parallelists

Sharon and Keith are not marriage partners but independent operators who happen to share the same living area. These two professionals find this working arrangement agreeable to their needs. Sharon, who makes $22,000 a year, does her own income tax, keeps her own checking account, and belongs to an investment club, independent of her husband. Keith, whose annual salary is $30,000, does the same as Sharon, but he invests his extra income in rental property, where he spends his weekends making needed repairs and improvements.

They each put $450 a month into the household fund and from that they pay their rent, food bills, and other joint expenses. They maintain their own cars, and if they see something the other might like, they buy it from their private funds and bring it home as a gift. Sometimes Keith takes Sharon out to dinner, but he doesn't do it more than twice unless Sharon takes him out to a place of her choice.

Such parallel living provides an ideal arrangement for these two. When Sharon and Keith do something for each other, they have their own money with which to do it. These two will never have the wretched quarrels that tore Don and Melissa's marriage apart. They have a businesslike partnership for joint expenses. Everything else is separate.

Monetary patterns are usually manifestations of natural tendencies that are expressed elsewhere as well. Keith and Sharon, in their orderly way, divide household chores without resentment or jealousy.

Sometimes they help each other, but it is clearly understood that if Keith helps Sharon with the dishes it is because he wants to, not because he has to. The dishes are her job. If she helps him clean the garage, it is out of generosity rather than a sense of duty. And some jobs they specifically prefer to do alone, unaided and uninterrupted. They have separate closets and separate bathrooms, and they solved their pet problem in characteristic style. She has a canary and he a tank of tropical fish.

The Uniteds

Joe and Wanda's arrangement represents the most common type of two-career marriage. Wanda has a part-time job that pays $5,500 a year. She works only in the mornings because she and Joe decided that while their two children were growing up it would be good if one of them could be home when the children came back from school. Joe makes $33,000, and they put both salaries in a single joint checking account. At the beginning of each month they put what's left from the previous month's balance into their joint savings account.

Since Joe is busy with his career, Wanda takes responsibility for household buying, except for large items like furniture and appliances. They shop together for these, assuming that half the fun is in the choosing. Since both are fairly easygoing about money, they defer to the other if it is clear that one of them *really* wants something. Joe, for example, thought it was foolish for Wanda to pay $175 for a food processor, but he decided that if Wanda felt the gadget was necessary for modern living, he would go along with her.

Joe and Wanda are realistic about money, even though they are easygoing. They recognize it as a limited resource to be used as intelligently as possible so they can derive maximum joint benefit from it. Neither of them has extravagant tastes, and they are sure that they can enjoy themselves without having to spend money doing it. Their family entertainment consists largely of picnics, camping, and simple activities that cost little while renewing their energy.

If two people are rational, they can be "uniteds," even though one or the other has financial weaknesses. Shortly after Kay married Mark, she discovered that he had no sense of money management and no intention of developing one. Although he made good money, he spent it all—and then some. He would take four or five friends out for the evening and buy them dinner and drinks, either with a charge card or a check.

After her initial panic subsided, Kay convinced Mark that he should relinquish control of the family purse. He gave up his charge cards and put the checking account in Kay's name. Now she gives him lunch money just as she gives it to the children; and if he asks her for something extra, she questions him about it before she gives him the money.

Kay and Mark have been married for over ten years and the system is still working nicely. Mark never gets angry at Kay's fiscal decisions. He laughs and says, "We both know I can't hold on to anything, and somebody's got to take care of the family. I'm lucky Kay's not the same way I am."

If you accept the united attitude toward family money, then the next question has to be "Which one can manage it better?" Only by examining your own personalities can you figure out who that will be. Like most couples, you will probably find that one partner is more careful and conscientious with money than the other. If both of you tend toward prodigality, you have to work together to fight your natural casualness.

No matter what your joint income is, it is a good idea to have a monthly budget that sets aside special allowances for each of you to spend separately. That way you can buy things for yourself and presents for others without feeling guilty, since you have the final say over a certain amount of money in the family.

All of us need to feel that some money is clearly ours. Once it has been deposited in the family coffers and transferred to our name, no matter what its original source, we have a clear title to it. Although we may consult with each other about our money, we are responsible for its final disposition, and we don't have to account to anyone for its use.

MONEY PRESSURES FROM PEERS

In addition to the pressures of money management at home, financial pressures from outside the family can cause trouble in a marriage unless they are dealt with realistically. In our professions we associate with people in a wide salary range. What some regard as essentials could be extravagances for us. We should never let peer pressure blur the distinction between necessary spending and prestige spending. Such confusion destroys budgets and threatens our happiness.

Una and Herb are an example. As regional manager for a chain of women's clothing stores, Una worked with the managers of branch outlets to determine their stock needs for each season. She felt it was important to dress well in her job. Herb was in a construction business and wore khakis most of the year. He liked Una to be well dressed, but he told her frequently that he thought she spent more than she should on clothes.

"I have to look good in business," she said. "You can't have a regional manager looking dowdy. And, anyway, I get a 25 percent discount on everything."

Herb was still not convinced. For a year he kept a record of the money Una spent on clothes and found that she spent $700 more than she brought home. Even Una, as much as she liked to dress, was impressed with Herb's statistics. "Maybe I had just run low," she argued at first. "This was probably not a typical year." But she thought about her situation and realized that she was working for nothing. "No," she disagreed with her own thought, "I'd have to have clothes anyway."

As she and Herb continued their discussion, they came to see that she had taken the job in women's clothing because of a natural interest in that area. As she advanced in management, she became more and more fashion conscious, so that she was never satisfied with what she had. The combination of her natural taste and her job pressured her into a state of continuous sartorial dissatisfaction.

Herb and Una resolved their problem by having Una take a position for less money with a fast-food chain where the pressure to dress well was not so great. To Una's surprise, she did not immediately recover from her preoccupation with appearance. She was in the habit of buying clothes and couldn't easily change. She even imposed her interest on the people at work by constantly talking about fashion and her previous job. "It's like alcoholism," she told Herb. "You just don't get over it right away. Even when I tell myself I'm thinking about clothes too much, I'm still thinking about clothes. What can I do?"

Herb was not the inflammatory type. "You'll get over it," he said, "when you find something more interesting to think about." And it was true. After about six months, Una was talking about her new job with the same vigor that she had devoted to clothes before.

Some people, like Una, are especially susceptible to outside pressures. In her new job Una became as conscious of food as she had previously been of clothes. She needed to excel in whatever seemed important, and her values were determined largely by the corporation for which she worked.

Her devotion to her company made her an extremely successful manager, but it also interfered with her private life. Although Herb was patient, he occasionally grew so tired of hearing her repeat career clichés that he stopped listening to her.

All of us are susceptible to public pressures. Since we want to have the things others have, we are likely to accumulate tastes beyond our means. Without knowing it, we expand our material expectations until they outrun our budget. One two-career family has monthly credit installments totaling $700 more than their combined monthly income. The payments cover a series of luxury items that they bought as a result of conversations with their manager friends. At first, they controlled their greed. But once they succumbed to the buying urge, it ruined them. Here is the way it worked.

Rose came home one day and said, "We really can't eat well at home without a microwave oven. Mr. Wells was telling us today that his wife has one, and it is a great time saver."

"We can't afford one of those," Hank said. But a few weeks later he brought the subject up again. "Funny, you know. We were talking about microwave ovens only the other day. One of the men at work bought his wife one for their anniversary. He says for working couples it's the only way to go." And soon they were experimenting with their new microwave oven.

The pattern continued. They didn't enjoy their vacation that year because Hank's boss had told him how much they were going to spend on motels. Why didn't they buy themselves a camper and save the motel expenses? They could cook in the camper too. Soon they had a camper that stood in the driveway most of the year because it was too high to fit in the garage. A motorboat was parked to one side of it and a sailboat in the yard behind.

Although Hank and Rose scorned TV advertisements as cheap commercialism, they were the victims of a far more insidious peer pressure advertising. Their lives were incomplete unless they had the same things as those around them. Since they worked with managers in the $100,000-a-year bracket, they tried to tell themselves that they could never have all the things their associates had. They wanted them, though, and continued to buy them until their installment payments became as unrealistic as their materialistic dreams.

Spending money doesn't necessarily make us happy. Hank and Rose were more wretched when their driveway was full of toys than when the driveway was empty and they were free of debt. They didn't buy to enjoy their purchases but to keep up with their peers. They made the mistake of thinking that it was the camper and the boat and the microwave oven that made the people who talked them into buying these things happy people. Actually, the people they talked to were simply sharing their own pleasures with Hank and Rose, not trying to sell them something. It would have been far better if Hank and Rose had made a realistic appraisal of what they could afford and settled for enjoying that.

Still, it is difficult to endure the feeling of inferiority that sometimes comes from money pressures exerted on us by the people around us at work. It is easy to believe that club memberships, airplanes, condominiums in Aspen or Vale, and trips to the Bahamas are what money is for. Actually, money is for freeing us from the necessity of letting someone else control our lives. When we learn to control our money, we can be free of the public pressures to spend as others spend. Our personal needs, not what others think we should do with our money, ought to determine our purchasing choices.

PRIVATE MONEY PRESSURES

We are frequently as pressured from within ourselves as we are from external financial sources. Peer pressure is often less persistent and intense than this internal pressure—feelings of guilt, inadequacy, and jealousy. These feelings need to be identified so we can deal with them.

Guilt
Most of us carry a sizable burden of guilt—moral, sexual, or spiritual. Advertising, religion, the opinions of relatives and friends sometimes aggravate our sense of guilt. In our mercantile tradition, we

try to buy back our innocence with money. We give to our church, charities, our family, and sometimes even to ourselves in the belief that we can thus expiate the numerous sins in our secret souls.

We can feel guilty about anything from a love affair to a forgotten birthday. With our families, we feel especially guilty that we haven't provided more of everything. As the children grow older, we regret that we haven't given them more time, more attention, more advantages. One man, playing with his five-year-old daughter in her sandbox on his afternoon off, admitted that he felt ashamed the whole time he was there because he had waited so long to play with her. Such feelings are common to most of us.

While Phil and Theresa were still in college, they had two children. Phil's older brother, who had finished medical school and was established in a practice, bought his children expensive toys and equipment that Phil and Theresa couldn't afford. Phil's parents often commented on how sad it was that Phil's children didn't have the advantages their cousins did.

As Phil and Theresa's children grew up, the family income increased. By the time the children were in high school their parents began lavishing luxuries on them to compensate for the things they hadn't been able to give them in the early years. Both children spurned the luxuries and rejected the colleges their parents wanted for them.

Phil talked to his brother about his disappointment in his children. "Why are they so uninterested in making their way in life?" he asked. "We've certainly tried to give them the most we could as long as we've been able to. Is it because they had a disadvantage early in their lives?"

"No," the brother said, "you gave to your children because *you* wanted them to have things. I gave to mine because I thought it was good for *them* to have things. You were thinking of yourself; I was thinking of the children."

It took Phil a while to understand the difference, but the point his brother was trying to make was that family expenditures should not be governed by a selfish motive such as the alleviation of guilt. Buying things for our children to make ourselves feel better is never a sound reason for spending money.

Inadequacy

Our feeling of inadequacy is related to our sense of guilt. Feeling our incompleteness, we want to fill it out with money. Calvin and Phyllis are an example. Calvin became a vice president in his bank without having finished college. Unlike the other officers, he came from a poor family with few cultural advantages and he couldn't forget it. He succeeded through a bullheadedness that actually covered deep inferiority feelings.

Soon after he moved into his first good position, he swore he would never have his wife and children suffer the material deprivation he had. Each of his three children got a car and a trip to Europe for high school graduation. Phyllis had a pool in the backyard and a fur coat in the closet. She continued to work in spite of Calvin's disapproval. "I need to have something to do besides sit around here and take your money," she said. "This way I feel that something of what we spend comes from me."

Calvin's mother had worked simply to keep her children in shoes, so that for Calvin a working woman was a sign of failure in the husband. He could not conceive of any other reason for a wife to work. At the same time, his sense of inadequacy kept him from disagreeing with Phyllis. Phyllis made most of the decisions—other than the financial ones—because Calvin was living in a world so alien from his background. Unsure how to respond to the new world's demands, he relinquished control to Phyllis.

The only area in which he could express himself was in giving gifts to his family. He refused to surrender that right. When Phyllis wondered if it would be wise to give one of the children something, Calvin's immediate reaction was "I had to do without that when I was a boy. I don't want my children to have to suffer the way I did."

One of the dangers when inadequacy is a motive for family spending is the expectation of gratitude. Calvin derived no joy from the money he spent on his wife and children because they did not give him as much appreciation as he wanted. The gifts meant a great deal more to him than to the people who received them. He would have been overjoyed with a car, a trip to Europe, a stereo, or a college education. But for his children these things were simply another item in a long list of luxuries that they had not asked for.

Money spent to compensate for inadequacy, like money spent to absolve guilt, is rarely spent for others. These emotionally motivated expenditures may satisfy us for the moment, but the emotion is in charge. If we recognize the motives behind our family expenditures, we can usually control them. Often, it is easier for our partners to recognize our motives than it is for us. When they do, they need to find a tender, loving way to point out poor motives to us.

Jealousy

Like the other emotional pressures from within us, jealousy is usually unconscious and therefore uncontrolled. It may arise from the immediate family or from the extended family.

Financial jealousy between husband and wife is a common phenomenon. Some couples compete either in spending on themselves or in spending on their children to win their affection and love. Ken felt that Laura spent more than she should on clothes. Laura was sure that Ken spent more than his share on sports. They depleted their bank account because each was convinced that the other was prodigal in the wrong areas. "I'm making almost as much as she does," Ken said. "I have a right to spend money the way I want to."

Laura decided, "He's the head of the household. I make my money to spend on myself. It's his job to support me. He has no money sense whatever. What he wants, he buys. Why shouldn't I do the same thing?"

Such jealousy will make a financial chaos out of a family budget unless it is recognized and controlled. The only way to manage money, in a business or in a family, is rationally. We have a number of choices, and we must consider these choices and make the best ones we can, independent of guilt, inadequacy, or jealousy.

Internal financial pressures are always present. We would all like to have more, but our budgets are limited. By accepting our financial limitations, we can learn ways of spending what we have to obtain the most for our money. After a few years of careful control we will derive more pleasure from wise money management than from poor spending habits.

THE LONG VIEW

One of our friends who inherited a family fortune asked us how you can tell whether it is money that is cementing your marriage. We suggested a simple test for determining how dependent your marriage is upon that most powerful product of your public and private existence—money. It consists of a single question: "Do I spend my money emotionally or rationally?"

This chapter has suggested ways to move toward rational family spending. None of us is totally free of a dependence on money for our emotional fulfillment, but we can work toward liberation from expecting money to do things it can't do. We learn what money can do by breaking our total financial picture up into small views and examining them in terms of our present situation and our future possibilities.

Expenses

Pete and Mimi made a combined salary of $45,000, but they never had enough money for the bills. "We don't have to make a million dollars," Pete said year after year, "but we want to live as if we had it." And Mimi topped him with "Our debts are our major assets." They had the same sanguine attitude toward their expenses. They pretended they didn't exist. Secretly, though, they both worried a lot about them. They could not find a way to limit their spending to a reasonable approximation of their income.

Their attitude toward expenses was really an admission of lack of control. They spent when they had money and credit, did without when money and credit were gone. Neither of them had a clear sense of how to budget their income. Their children were fearful and insecure because of their parents' persistent financial incompetence.

Next to these prodigal parents were the frugal ones. Paul and Bertha squeezed every penny that ever came in and saved half of it. They didn't enjoy anything because it always cost more than it should have. They developed the desperate look of the couple in Grant Wood's *American Gothic* and spent most of their time talking about how much they had saved.

Both the frugals and the prodigals had an emotional attitude toward their family expenses. They should have worked out some long-range projection about their present and future needs, then developed a program that would take care of next year's taxes and insurance with a little left over for an emergency fund. The realistic approach demands persistent attention and perpetual adjustment. Expenses are something that can't be ignored. Unless you cope with them, they can make your life miserable. You have to find out what choices you have and then learn to live with them.

Investments

Every family needs a little something left over. Even in the years when expenses are at their highest, you should try to put a little money into a safe investment program. You don't have to be like the frugals, but you do have to accept the inevitability of financial limitations at home, as you do at work.

In the area of investments a strange split sometimes occurs between the public and the private world. Melanie worked as an accountant and Frank was a personnel officer in a bank. Both worked all day, managing other people's money and discussing budget situations. In their private life, though, they were inept with their funds. They kept saying to each other, "We really ought to work out some investment program," but they never got around to it. They excused themselves by saying that once they got the furniture and paid for the cars, they would save.

But it was always something else. Gradually they stopped talking about investments. When their friends discussed financial topics, Melanie and Frank did not even look at each other, but sat quietly, contributing nothing to the conversation. They felt ashamed and noncommunicative about investments. Melanie thought it was Frank's job to work something out, and Frank did not have the time or the interest to do it. After all, he thought, Melanie is the financial expert in the family.

Their failure to incorporate their public knowledge into their private life made them insecure and weakened their marriage. Family security requires a realistic savings program. Except for those first months of marriage, when expenditures are likely to exceed income, we all need an investment program. What that program is depends on our own abilities and preferences—real estate investment, stocks, government notes, mutual funds. As managers of our private realm, we must become as knowledgeable as we can about investing and talk to each other about it. Investments do the same thing for a family that they do for a business—they secure its future.

Retirement

One reason for investing is to prepare for the day when our earning capacity declines to zero. Social Security is hardly enough for most retired families, and some supplementary income is necessary. Again, as with other financial considerations, we have to take a long-range, rational view of the future and work out a program that will provide what we need. Our mothers and fathers probably did their own retirement planning, but today many companies assume this burden for us. If our organization has a retirement program, we should become familiar with it and know what we will need to supplement it.

One of our friends discovered to his horror, when he was sixty-three, that his retirement program had no survivor benefits. Only then did he realize that his wife was unprovided for. Such surprises can be avoided by early investigation of retirement plans. Another friend was bound to his company because his retirement program was not a vested one. He put so much into the retirement plan that, at fifty-two, he had to refuse a good offer with another company because it would not match what he had in his present retirement plan.

Change

We are never too young to look all the way to the end of the road, because the end is bound to come. We don't need to spend all our time looking ahead, but we should glance up once in a while to make sure an unexpected change has not occurred. Change is something we cannot anticipate, but it is always in the economic picture. Buying power fluctuates from year to year, and the dollar rises and falls. We owe it to our families to remain alert to economic news and respond to it in a rational, unemotional way. The pressures in both our private and public lives will be lessened by constant vigilance.

If we learn to sense the rhythm of economic change, we can arrange our public and private lives in such a way that the choices are ours, not society's. We will come to know the pleasures of wise money management and the joy of family security.

The Joneses Talk About Money Management

Bill: Do you suppose everybody feels guilty and inadequate about money the way I do?

Ruth: I don't feel guilty and inadequate. You may feel that way because you make a lot. I think I am in control of what I spend. I may have many hidden desires and hang-ups, but I don't express them in the way I spend money.

Bill: How did you get that kind of control? I'm always wanting things I can't have and feeling both self-pity and self-disgust as a result of my materialistic longings.

Ruth: I know. You called me stingy the other day.

Bill: That was the highest compliment I could think of at the moment. I suppose stinginess goes along with guilt-free money management. Responsible management requires that you hold on to more than you spend. That's a lesson you're still trying to teach me.

Ruth: I don't think you're as bad at money management as you think you are. I learned to manage money the same way you did—by being taught it from an early age. You're on a psychological allowance, even when you seem to be extravagant. I've noticed that you may spend with prodigal abandon, but you always stop before you spend more than you should. I'm just more careful all the time.

Bill: We complement each other nicely. You're always putting on the brakes, and I'm always running downhill. But I wonder if people can really control and change their attitude toward money. Aren't some just naturally scatterbrained about it?

Ruth: It would seem so, but we know lots of people who live happily within their means, whose money is a joy to them, and who don't ache themselves out of envy for the things others have. This whole book assumes that financial scatterbrains can learn from people like that.

Bill: If you had to isolate the quality that makes these people capable of enjoying their money, what would you say it is?

Ruth: That they accept themselves for what they are rather than trying to be what other people expect them to be. As Shakespeare says, when you're not contented and are envious of others, you think of someone you really love and then you're happy. The mad search for material possessions is simply an inadequate substitute for love.

Bill: You summarize the sonnet nicely. We must assume that with loving understanding a couple can manage its finances. But without love, neither of them is going to derive much benefit from money in the long run. The next question: Can money be used to foster existing love or to cultivate it?

Ruth: It can be used to provide many advantages and happy times.

Bill: And happy times are really necessary for the continued growth of love. I'm convinced that poverty can stifle love if it goes on too long—and that goes for bad money management too. I've seen extremely poor people whose total energy has been invested in surviving. That doesn't leave much time for love. And I've seen people with quite a bit of money, who are still so obsessed about it that their love suffocates from lack of breathing space.

Ruth: Yes. I've known many rich people for whom money has stifled love. The love of money is not the soil in which human love grows best.

Bill: No. But the fact that we have come to the point at which love and money meet suggests that, as we have already said in this chapter, neither of these two powerful forces can be ignored in a healthy marriage.

11

Two-Career Time Control

IN two-career marriages managing time is often as difficult as managing money. Both are limited commodities that we never have enough of. Time is related to energy, and it is the expenditure of energy that we have to consider when we are trying to achieve a balanced use of time. If we could get by on three hours of sleep, we would have less trouble with time—we think. Achievers that we are, though, we would probably come to begrudge the three hours of sleep and try to cut it down to two and a half.

Differing energy levels are the cause of most time balance problems in two-career marriages. Just as members of a couple have different boiling points, so they have different energy levels. Trudy and Horace had a normal courtship that didn't reveal the trouble to come, but the indicators were present. They would go out on a date and dance till two in the morning. The next morning Trudy would be up for six o'clock mass and then jog till breakfast. Horace slept till noon on Sundays and then, with the help of two cups of coffee, watched TV until it was time to go to bed again.

After they were married, Trudy was totally unsympathetic with Horace's sluggish metabolism. "You're three times my size," she said. "You should have three times my energy."

"I'm three times your size, so I need three times as much sleep," he replied.

Since they both worked all week, Horace felt the weekend should be for rest. Trudy regarded it as an opportunity for vigorous play combined with household chores. Horace felt that Trudy bossed him and drove him; Trudy regarded Horace as a lazy killjoy. The trouble was that they did not understand the far-reaching consequences of their differing energy levels.

Even when people's energy levels are the same, time use can be a problem. When they married, Roy was in a one-year management training program and Ann worked as a secretary in a large typing pool. Since Roy brought work home at night and on weekends, Ann took over the responsibility for family financial dealings as well as the regular household tasks. Ann found her duties at home more stimulating than those at work. Roy, on the other hand, thought about his profession most of the time. In spite of their different interests, during these first years they made the most of the little time Roy took from his work. Going out for a hamburger or a movie was something special, because when they came home work was waiting for them both.

By the time Roy finished his internship, Ann was promoted to a managerial position that required more after-hours thought and preparation. She began to feel pressured and wondered why Roy didn't take over more of the jobs around the house. Why should he watch TV while she did the dishes? When the first child came along, Roy was anxious to help, but he didn't know how. Ann resented the way Roy watched her work until nine or ten every night. Roy, feeling guilty and sensing the tension, began going out to play cards or to have a drink with friends. "Just to relax," he said.

Had Ann and Roy redistributed their use of time at this point in their life, they could have continued to enjoy shared couple time. As it was, they underwent a temporal separation—each using time independent of the other and feeling excluded from the other's time. Roy would have much rather stayed home in the evenings, but it wasn't pleasant there. Ann was lonely without him, but she resented his inactivity while she was overworked in her "spare" time.

Two-career families have to maintain a high degree of flexibility about their investment of time because when they lose control of it they become its victims. Ambitious, intelligent people naturally feel that they can never achieve as much as they want. For the sake of their mental health, these people have to work out time management patterns that assure them a reasonable balance between their professional lives and their private existence.

CHUNKS OF TIME

Our naturally conservative personalities, combined with our submission to immediate demands, often lead to a strange warping of time. We willingly accept change in the world around us. We know that nations rise and fall, the dollar grows stronger or weaker, relationships with other countries improve or deteriorate. But in our personal lives, we tend to believe that the way things are is the way they will always be.

Our hopes and fears are a permanent background for the *right now* that is always with us. We have difficulty anticipating a drastic shift in our condition, for better or for worse. Early in their marriage Roy and Ann established a set pattern of time use and ignored changes which required time adjustments. We can avoid a similar mistake by identifying the major chunks of time in our lives and arranging them to suit our needs.

The First Bite

In the first years of marriage, as we've seen in earlier chapters, our balancing patterns are developing. These formative years are the ones when we bite off our first chunk of time for consumption. If we try to save it instead of using it immediately, we will lose the opportunity forever.

Trying to live in the future is the great danger of these first years. Even though we can't take a trip up the Amazon like our rich relatives, we can enjoy our couple time if we don't spend it wishing for something else. One young couple we know finishes every night with a fierce round of Chinese checkers. Another couple declares every long weekend off an official "home holiday." They outlaw any kind of work—yardwork, cleaning, or business—and treat their home for that weekend as a posh resort where they have no responsibility.

Futurism may be necessary for corporate planning, but for a couple it can lead to a dream world that detracts from the joy of the present. Sometimes it even spoils the future. Daryl and Vivian spent their time together during the first five years of marriage planning what wonderful things they would do when they had more money. They worked overtime to make sure they advanced more quickly than their competitors, and they developed the habit of living in the future. When the future finally came, they were the same driven, anxious people they had been before. Their vacations were more expensive now, but they had forgotten how to have fun. After the third year of success, Vivian ran off with a man who had less money than Daryl. "He may not be rich," she said, "but he knows how to show me a good time."

Good times are important at all stages of life. Sacrificing the first good times for the hope of better ones can build disappointment. Couples who know about balanced time management put part of their time into present enjoyment and part into realistic planning for the future.

Choice Cut

The central years of our career are as busy as the first ones, but now we spend our time in different ways. Committees, parties, and planned outings pile up so fast that we sometimes feel we have no control over time. For two-career people these years take their toll because separate career demands eat into shared couple time.

Even when couple time is available, it may come when one or both partners are so tired that the moment is unrewarding. Most of the time, two-career people see each other when they are exhausted. They get up together, rush around getting ready for work, and put in their best hours with other people. They come home to get a meal, take care of the children, and try to find some clean clothes for the next day.

Wes and Lottie went through a typical midcareer slump. They got into the habit of expressing their professional frustration and fatigue by carping at each other and their children. Instead of being a place of rest and quiet, their home became an explosives factory for pent-up emotions. They were considering divorce when their marriage counselor suggested relief shifts.

"What's a relief shift?" Wes asked.

"One week one of you gets the supper and does the dishes; the next week the other takes over those jobs," the counselor said. "That way you either have time off or are providing time off for somebody you love."

After a month of switching off jobs at home, Wes and Lottie found that their mood had changed. They had grown so interested in various combinations of relief shifts that what used to be a burden for them became a game.

Even at best, though, we have to learn to live with fatigue in these years. We cannot continue to act with youthful abandon unless we make some sacrifice for it. And we usually make this sacrifice in the sheltered, private portion of our lives. We are the hardhitting executive during the day, but at night we let down the strings of our emotional life. The family sees the worn-out self that we are trying to hide from others.

The best way to compensate for this fatigue is to allow ourselves more rest time. The organization will still be there no matter how many hours we give it each day. Learning ways of relaxing on the job will help us save part of our strength for our private lives. We don't have to be the liveliest participant in every committee meeting. By now we should know which meetings are important and which ones we can afford to miss without being missed. Along with our professional maturity should come an ability to distinguish useful activity from useless activity. By substituting intelligent experience for youthful vigor, we can make it happily through the center-cut years.

Brad and Rod worked for the same company and ran a competition course. Brad spent his time studying the power structure and doing his job so thoroughly that no one could find fault with him. Rod, the bright young thing, bounced around making golf dates with his superiors, organizing a charity bazaar, and setting up cocktail parties for visiting dignitaries. Brad went home in the evenings and put his work aside while he and his family lounged around the table laughing together. Rod took his wife out where they could be seen—to the club or to some office function.

Brad plodded on in his course. Rod's frantic activity drove his wife into a nervous breakdown and Rod into bouts of uncontrolled drinking. Even after Brad passed Rod by, Rod couldn't admit that he had used his time unwisely. He believed Brad had used some secret trick to get ahead. He summed it up one night in a moment of drunken truth when he shouted at Brad, "You've just got more energy than I have, you slimy schemer."

It wasn't Brad's energy that gained him professional success, but rather his basic wisdom. He knew how to conserve what time he had for useful tasks. Like a good distance runner, Brad knew how to kick with efficiency and minimum effort to get ahead without becoming winded. We all have the same amount of time. If we use it to advantage, our center-cut years will pay off in professional advancement and enriched family ties.

Tender Morsel

When the children have left home and the job is under control, we can laugh at the young ones who are making such a big fuss over matters that no longer concern us. If we have used our previous time wisely, these years are the payoff ones. We still have our health and vigor, and we have more time at our disposal than ever before. This new condition has its challenges, even as the earlier ones did. We have become so accustomed to running hysterically from place to place in our public and private lives that we continue to manufacture excuses for running. We accept useless committee assignments and dinner invitations that bore us, and we feel obliged to create an illusion of activity.

This period has been described as "the empty-nest syndrome." It is characterized by alternating periods of frantic activity and depressed inactivity. But it doesn't have to be that way. We are now exciting, mature people instead of thrill-seeking young adults, and we have more time for each other. The change can be an improvement if we take the time to get to know each other again.

Promotions and children come and go, but the single, steady center of our lives is the husband-wife relationship. We may have to make a formal effort to get to know each other again, much as if we were beginning the dating process once more. We can go out for the evening or have friends over the way we did in courtship.

At first this release from tension and responsibility can be disconcerting. We may be ill at ease because we no longer have an excuse for jumping up and dashing off. We are now mature enough, though, not to need excuses. If we find a party dull or a committee meeting useless, we can say politely, "I'm sorry, but I have to go now." After we have tried this exit line once or twice, we will experience a new joy. We've eaten our vegetables and have the dessert before us.

THE WORKWEEK

At every stage of life we need regular rhythms to help us survive. The medieval church, realizing the importance of patterns for structuring existence, organized time into the Holy Year. With never-varying cycles, time swung through commemorative seasons and culminated in Holy Week before Easter. In addition to this long view of time, the day was divided into canonical hours that marked its passing and contributed to its meaningfulness.

That rigid ordering of time is no longer appropriate, but we do need conveniently discernible patterns so that we can gain control over time. We develop a sense of progress by moving from one clearly anticipated point in time to another.

The basic time unit for most of us is the workweek. We build from a rested, industrious Monday through the "hump" on Wednesday to TGIF on Friday. Our emotional states follow this pattern. Monday, Wednesday, and Friday are the best days for talking to superiors because they too come under the cycle. They are likely to be placid on Monday, irritable on Tuesday, hopeful on Wednesday, tired on Thursday, and relieved on Friday.

Even people who like their work are subconsciously responsive to this general pattern in American business life. Most two-career families have the advantage of sharing the same workweek schedule. Our highs and lows come together so that we are sympathetic with each other on Tuesday night and celebrate on Friday. This pattern seems so natural to us that when we hear of someone working the midnight shift or going to work on Saturday afternoon, we are shocked to realize that our work pattern is not the only one in the world.

These weekly rhythms are necessary for psychic survival. Couples who violate the order of the workweek often pay for it. Ray was a field representative for a men's wear chain, and Doris managed the local outlet of the same chain. Their common professional interest formed the basis of their marriage.

At first their lives were enriched by their shared attitudes toward the organization. But after several years together, they developed different workweeks. Ray could schedule his appointments at any time he pleased and had no regular hours. Sometimes he would sleep until noon; at other times he would be up fixing his breakfast at five o'clock. His clients liked to see him on Sunday mornings or Saturday afternoons over cocktails. Doris had regular hours, like most of the people she and Ray knew. As a result, they had little social life. She couldn't count on Ray to be free on Friday evening, Saturday, or any other specific time, so she was unable to make definite social commitments.

When Ray was able to sleep till noon, he would stay up watching late-night television and drinking beer until two or three in the morning. These irregularities irritated Doris. She was jealous of Ray's freedom and resentful of his intrusion on the regularity of her life. Without knowing it, Ray was expressing his antisocial tendencies by exploiting his differences from those who had to work regular hours.

As Doris' irritation became obvious, Ray increased his efforts to demonstrate his freedom from the usual workweek pattern. Once he scheduled all his appointments for Saturday and Sunday and went skiing the rest of the week. "Too bad," he said to Doris, "that your schedule won't allow you the flexibility that mine does, but I'm sure you don't begrudge me a little fun once in a while. When I work, I really work hard."

Their marriage was at the point of dissolution when Ray, honestly anxious to save it, talked Doris into going to a marriage counselor. The counselor's solution was simple. She suggested that Ray and Doris coordinate their workweek so that they could spend their leisure time together. As they worked out this new pattern with the aid of the counselor, Ray's insecurity, which had been the major cause of his antisocial attitude, disappeared. He became agreeable to the same pattern that most of the rest of the world followed. When anyone asked him to schedule something on Saturday afternoon, he would smile and say, "Can't we find another time? After all, some things are sacred, aren't they?"

The workweek, like so many other aspects of a two-career marriage, is significant without being particularly noticeable. Until we become aware of the necessity for regulating it, we are its unwilling victims. Once we accept the inevitability of a design in our professional life, we can create our own pattern for free time.

THE DAILY GRIND

Sometimes it seems the day will never end; at other times the day is not long enough. Most of us are extremely conscientious and want to do our best in everything. We want the best children, the cleanest house, the greenest yard, the highest salary. This desire for supremacy makes us feel the pressures of grindstone days. Even without fighting our natural tendency to do well, we can control our daily activity so that it doesn't destroy the order of our lives. Here are four ways to gain control of our time.

Discriminating

Gerald runs up and down the office stairs from eight-thirty till five making contacts, carrying messages, and checking statistics. He flips frantically from one task to another. Someone calls him to see if he will be corresponding secretary for his civic club. Of course he will! When he gets home at night, his two children ask him to play ball with them. "I'm sorry," he says. "I've worked too hard today. I don't have the energy. Maybe tomorrow night." And when his wife asks him to take the garbage out, he says, "Let one of the children do it. I'm too tired."

Gerald could discriminate among the activities that are offered him, but he hasn't yet developed that ability. One of the hardest managerial jobs is learning to say no to inferiors and superiors. Successful people know how to distinguish between valuable activity and useless activity. The drudge has not cultivated this critical faculty and is continually beaten down by indiscriminate acceptance of whatever comes along. His priority list is determined by what comes first during the day.

If a useless task is scheduled from ten to twelve in the morning, we have to learn to conserve our energy for important activities in the afternoon and evening. We cannot afford to let the clock be our major discrimination tool; our own judgment must be our guide. Gerald's mistake was that he let external conditions make his decisions for him.

Knowing what is really important during the day is not always easy. We tend to deemphasize the private area of our lives and give all we have to our professional activities. Only the most naive beginner in management, though, believes that everything that happens at the office is critically important. The person who lavishes hours of research on an office memo that will be glanced at and thrown into the trash is wasting his energy. To spend an entire morning preparing for a three-minute presentation to a committee whose members have already made up their minds is equally fruitless.

Wise managers apportion the day's work by estimating the energy output for each activity and saving a little for unexpected strains. They maintain a balance that leaves them something besides an empty carcass to drag home at night.

Maintenance of good private relationships is, after all, the main reason for our involvement in public affairs. We know one manager who says to every luncheon invitation, "I'm sorry, but I can't make it. I have to go home to walk the dog. He needs me worse than you do." With that attitude, this manager will survive a long time.

Conciliating

The manager with the dog did more than differentiate. He handled his allocation of time in such a way that others did not take offense. We must discriminate in a conciliatory way, so that no one can be offended. Conciliation can take either a direct or an indirect form. With both approaches, our purpose is the same—to keep people happy while we protect ourselves from exploitation.

The direct approach to conciliation is the easy one. We engage in no subterfuge; we simply say we're sorry but we can't. After this opening we have several choices:

1. We can explain that we are pushed to the wall and that we would like very much to take on this new opportunity, but it's not possible right now. We can use any number of excuses—our partner has made us promise not to take on any new jobs; it isn't permitted by our contractual arrangement with the organization; we have refused seven other people and wouldn't feel right about accepting now. Our explanation should make it clear to the petitioner that we wish him well and care enough to construct an elaborate excuse to go along with the rejection.

2. If we really don't want to be bothered again, we can respond truculently, suggesting that we have been insulted by an offer that is obviously beneath us. We are accustomed to a professionalism that has not been exhibited here and are deeply offended.

3. We can reject our petitioner with extreme humility, making it clear that we would like to undertake the job but are totally inferior to its demands. This kind of directness can be so emotionally devastating that the petitioner will blush and turn away quickly, ashamed that he

ever approached us. Afterward he will regard us as someone special —a humble manager.

Indirect conciliation is more difficult and requires some imagination. As with direct rejection, our purpose is to conserve our time for something better, but here we cannot afford to leave a negative impression. The classic example is the manager who was invited by his boss to the compulsory office garden party. He did not go, but he carefully made a point of saying to the boss the next time he saw him, "As usual, your party was perfect."

The boss, thinking of something else, said, "Oh, I didn't see you there."

"Well, you can't be expected to remember everybody when you have such a good turnout," the time saver replied.

As this example demonstrates, there are two cardinal rules in indirect conciliation: you don't refuse and you don't lie directly, although you consciously create a false positive impression. The idea is to save your time and still come out a winner.

All of us slip into conciliatory patterns without realizing it. In a moment of excessive generosity we say, "I'll bring you my copy of last month's report; it's at home on my desk. Oh, no, it won't be any trouble at all." Then we forget completely about bringing the report. Since most people are too polite to ask, that is the end of the demand on our time and thought.

Obviating

When we have cultivated the first two time-saving techniques, we can move on to the third, which is dependent on them. Having learned how to discriminate and conciliate, we can now decide which of our tasks are unnecessary and put them aside. One of the nicest ways to give ourselves an illusion of leisure is to look over our calendar each morning and decide on one activity that we don't need to do—then cancel it.

Our professional life is probably the easiest area to omit some daily task, because the red tape of corporate existence make a lot of activity redundant. In our home life obviating is a bit more difficult, since our presence there is so essential. Still, we should not view every activity as compulsory. Suppose we don't go to the little league game with our son. He arranges for a ride with someone else and learns the virtue of self-reliance. The same applies to our activities in the community. If we don't go to the political meeting, we don't get appointed secretary to the state convention and save ourselves not only time that day but three days in the future as well.

Time-saving is not just a negative pastime, of course. We are actually saving time for something better, even if that "something better" is the cultivation of a sense of leisure that makes everything else more pleasant. A trip to Europe is fun if we see one cathedral a day, but the whole trip can become a horror show if we schedule five or seven.

More important than the sense of leisure is the control we develop over our lives when we start jettisoning unnecessary items out of our daily flights. Our buoyancy will return, and we'll feel young again, because feeling young is mostly a matter of thinking we have all the time in the world to accomplish what we want in life. While we are obviating, we also need to maintain a reasonable balance between public and private life. We should not cut everything out of our private life so that we can have a sense of leisure in our public one. Unconscious pressures and biases may throw us off balance.

Scott hated his job so much that he began missing committee meetings and going home early. Craig hated his family so much that he stayed late at the office every night. Neither of these men was in control because neither recognized why he was doing his unbalancing act. If we hate our job or our marriage, we should admit it and then arrange things accordingly. We're happier when we know what we're doing, even if our motive is resentment.

Collaborating

The best way to alleviate the daily grind in two-career families is through cooperative living. This technique can be so effective that neither partner thinks he is doing any work. Dishes are an outstanding example. If one of us leaves the table and sits waiting for the other to finish the job, then one is wasting time and the other is putting in drudgery time. If we both clear the table and share the washing and putting away, then drudgery becomes a time of positive companionship.

We should look around the house for other ways to save time through collaboration. Clint and Evelyn were on the verge of divorce because Clint said Evelyn could not get ready to go places on time. He had developed the habit of going out to the car as soon as he was ready and sitting there in a sulk until she came out. Being a woman of some spirit, Evelyn loitered more and more to irritate him. After a few years they couldn't go anywhere together without a full-blown fight on the way.

With a little counseling, they tried collaboration. They set a specific time to get to the car, and before that time each was to participate in the preparations for departure. Clint, who was more compulsive than Evelyn, got ready and then went around the house making sure the doors were locked, the stove turned off, the lights out in the basement. In fact, he was taking over some of the chores that he had left for Evelyn to do while he had sat in the car sulking. Going places became fun again because they were each contributing to the departure.

Although collaboration is most easily initiated at home, we can establish a collaborative pattern with our colleagues. Collaboration creates a positive attitude rather than a critical one. We can answer the phone for an overworked receptionist instead of standing around fuming. Our voluntary cooperation makes it clear that everyone at work has the same aim—to make the office function efficiently.

Collaboration, like the other methods of alleviating the daily grind, requires a positive, trusting attitude. We must assume that most people mean well and are trying to do the right thing. When we run across someone who doesn't conform to this pattern, we should try to neutralize his negativism.

TIME TO RISE

Time will eventually kill us, but before that happens we can give it a pretty good fight. Organization is good battle strategy. By establishing a sense of order in our week and in our day, we can get control over the unruly enemy.

Generally, both at home and at work, we should cultivate a daily rhythm that we find comfortable. For most of us, this rhythm usually involves slowing down a bit, since we tend to run faster and faster. But the general pace should be constant and one at which we feel easy. When it gets too hectic, we make mistakes and our efficiency goes down. By choosing a suitable rhythm for ourselves and sticking to it, we can decelerate the pace of our lives.

If we have buckled under to time in the past, we need to make an effort to change our ways. Time, as much as money, is responsible for the happiness or the sorrow of living. Most of us tend to live either in the future or in the past. We need to focus on the present. Now is where we are, with present human relations, present problems, and present possibilities. Time will give us more of all of these, but we will cope with future choices better by handling the present ones first.

The Joneses Talk About Time

Bill: Let's talk a bit about time coordination in two-career marriages. You and I have found that we have to orchestrate our lives carefully to get everything in. Do you have any suggestions about how couples can accomplish that? In our own daily life, for example, does one of us have to take the primary scheduling responsibility?

Ruth: For both of us a good part of the day is scheduled by our jobs. For the rest of the day, because we want to spend time together, we have to plan. In a way this may restrict our freedom, but I think the benefits are well worth it. I would rather, for example, go to the grocery store while you're having a conference with one of your clients than wait until you've finished and then go.

Bill: What do you mean about the conference?

Ruth: I mean we should do our separate activities at the same time to have a maximum amount of time together.

Bill: I think one reason we have controlled time fairly well is that we have always placed our companionship above nonessential activities. I begrudge every minute I don't get to spend with you and the children. But I'm sure there are some happy marriages where the choices are not as clearcut as mine are.

Ruth: Yes. A marriage may work well when people have divided interests, but couples are usually happiest if both members agree about the choices. Remember my friend who was happy her husband was gone on the weekend so she could clean the house? And I gather he was glad to be gone. That was a happy marriage with time spent separately. Now that I think about it, several of my friends are quite satisfied to have time without their husbands. One retired woman I know told me, "I married him for better or worse, but not for lunch."

Bill: I suppose, in time coordination of the sort we're discussing, most couples adjust a little bit before marriage and continue to adjust afterward. If one member of the couple really has interests that take him away, the other either develops interests to fill that vacancy or grows resentful at being left alone.

Ruth: Time cannot really be separated from recreation, social life, education, and money. Time is the raw material out of which these products are made.

Bill: Yes, and the trouble is that we all work in an inflationary economy where we feel pressured to produce more and more. The best way to conserve time is not to deplete it by making useless products. We both know couples who knock themselves out doing things neither of them enjoys. How would you advise them to clear out time-wasting activities?

Ruth: By being honest with each other in a nonjudgmental way about what each really enjoys or feels is necessary. But I'd like to raise another question. How do you keep from going through life with a furrowed brow and the constant feeling that hurry as you may you're not going to finish all you have to do?

Bill: Pacing is the only answer to that persistent problem. We must accept the limits time places on us and pace ourselves so that we don't feel rushed. I think we can accomplish more, sometimes, if we don't push ourselves beyond an efficient running speed. Haste makes waste. It's a truism in any activity.

12

Satisfaction
or
Dissatisfaction

IN the Middle Ages, people saw themselves as creatures strapped to Fortune's wheel, which sometimes swirled them up to heavenly heights and then down into the depths. This fatalistic view of life took responsibility out of their hands and left them under the control and guidance of two powerful organizations—the church and the state. Today, our world view assumes a much larger area of free choice. We have many options, but these options sometimes generate fears and value conflicts that lead to discontent and a lingering malaise. Such negative feelings sap us of the energy we need to make wise choices. This chapter investigates the major causes of dissatisfaction and frustration in our lives.

Ellie and Ross thought they had their lives under control, but they are still plagued by dissatisfaction. For most of their adult lives they have fought against the present with perpetual scowls on their faces. When they married twenty years ago, Ellie told Ross that more than anything in the world she wanted a home and family just like the one she came from. Her mother's life was her model. Ellie spent her time diligently copying out recipes and taking care of her two babies. Ross was ambitious and anxious to advance up the corporate ladder. He worked in the evenings and on the weekends, leaving Ellie free to work in the kitchen.

While they were engaged in these separate activities, they kept wondering if they were doing what they wanted to be doing. Their conversations were largely anguished self-analysis. So many of Ellie's friends were out making money that she felt she was wasting her life at home. Ross's best friend from college was a professor who sneered at Ross's commercialism and opportunistic striving. Ellie and Ross lay awake at night wondering if they had made a terrible mistake.

When the children started school, Ellie got a job with a real estate firm. She showed houses in the afternoons and evenings. She resented being away from her family, but most of the other women in her neighborhood had jobs, and she felt she should have one too. Ross now held a senior managerial position with his company and did a lot of professional entertaining. Ellie resented having to help with that too. She wondered why she wasn't free to live her own life instead of helping Ross with his. He felt, in turn, that since he provided a good salary, Ellie should be willing to contribute to their home life.

As the children moved into adolescence, Ellie and Ross blamed each other openly for neglecting them. "It's your job to discipline them," Ellie said to Ross. "That's a father's task. I'm too busy with my work to bother about correcting them. And when are you going to teach them the value of money? They go through it without any awareness of how hard it is to earn."

After twelve years of accusations over the running of the house, Ellie told Ross she wanted a divorce. Ross said he didn't care, but he was too busy at the moment to bother with one. They'd see to it after a while. Time dragged on, and they forgot the divorce. Ellie began seeing a psychiatrist recommended by one of her clients. Ross spent a lot of time talking to his preacher and serving on church committees. Both of them felt smug, but the gnawing dissatisfaction remained. They are still trying very hard to do the right thing, but they are never quite sure what the right thing is.

Ellie and Ross are suffering from many of the afflictions that can accompany a two-career marriage. They are well-meaning, intelligent people, but they have failed. Their failure is not the result of an inability to make choices, because they have made many of them. Their mistake lies in not having developed a sound basis for making choices. At each stage in their lives they have been dissatisfied because they did not establish a clear value system to guide them.

CONFLICTS OF VALUES

Few people continue to want the same thing throughout their life, and sometimes these shifts in purpose cause a questioning of all values. The child takes his value system almost wholly from his parents. At that point he has no doubts about his values. They are shared by his sole authorities and himself. His world, therefore, is secure.

As his world expands, he modifies that system through his experiences with people of his generation. Thus he gradually composes his own set of values, independent of those his parents have given him. During this modification period, though, the parental value system often clashes with the new one. Here is an example.

Stephen Hart came from a small-town aristocracy that ruled the local church and reached strong lines out into state politics. Stephen's father and grandfather held uncompromisingly to the Protestant work ethic. Honesty, integrity, and hard work had made their construction business what it was—something to fear and respect. Stephen grew up in this strict, commercially oriented household, convinced that he had a safe place in a stable world.

Although his grandfather had not gone to college and his father had gone to the state university, one of Stephen's high school teachers convinced him that he was too smart for ordinary education, so Stephen enrolled in an Ivy League school. There he tried to apply his family's value system. He worked so hard for the first two years that he had a nervous breakdown.

Stephen came home and did some thinking while he was recovering his mental health. He had seen that those who succeeded at school were not the ones who worked hard but the ones who knew how to ingratiate themselves with their professors. The crassness of the student-professor relationship shocked Stephen, but he was success-oriented enough to want to adopt the system too.

When he went back to school, he imitated the new values that he had observed in operation. He talked his way into the right circles and was soon having tea on Sunday afternoon with the professors who had given him C's when he worked hard for them as a nonentity.

By the time he graduated, Stephen had discarded all his family values except the major one—he was going to succeed. He came home with a rich wife he had met at school and set himself the task of remaking Hart Construction Company. He fought with his father and grandfather and finally got his own way by setting the two against each other. Ten years later he was indicted by the state for bribing the highway department to get construction contracts.

A good lawyer won the case for him, and he is still building up his business, much to his parents' shame. His rich wife has left him, but he has another wife and several outside sexual attachments. His circle of friends is large and greedy. At forty-three, Stephen is deeply dissatisfied and wonders why he should be. He has everything he ever wanted. What else could there possibly be? His parents and his education convinced him that professional success was the way to happiness. Either you got it by hard work or you got it by scheming, but you got it.

Neither family influence, educational experience, nor professional life suggested to Stephen that values, like good clothes, must be suited to the individual. They are not bought ready-made off the rack and worn out of the store. Success, someone should have told Stephen, comes from considered evaluation of the lives of those around us. From them we can discover the professional and personal fulfillment that we seek. Stephen snatched at values the way he snatched at success in education and business, with no thought for his lasting satisfaction or that of others.

It is easy to see where Stephen went wrong, but not so easy, in midstream, to see where we are going wrong so that we can make adjustments in our course. At each stage of life we have to know why we are making the choices we make and establish priorities that will help us choose.

KNOWING WHY

As we free ourselves of other people's values and establish a set of our own, we develop self-awareness. Knowing why we make choices increases our control of life. Samuel Johnson's novel *Rasselas* tells of a prince who lived in Happy Valley, where everything was provided for him. He escaped into the outside world because he wanted a "choice of life." Free choice is what provides lasting satisfaction.

Our choices are often influenced by the fact that "everybody else is doing it." We follow the crowd by getting married at the *right* age, having children at the *right* age, even dying at the *right* age. If we are rebellious, we are just as strongly influenced by what everyone else is doing—and then we do the opposite. But life is not a column of numbers that must add up to something right. There is no right answer, just the best answer—for us. And for all of us that answer always involves feeling satisfied with what we are now doing and not living with regrets for the past or fears for the future.

Our motives for past actions, as much as the actions themselves, tell us how we make choices. Do we want approval from others? Do we want financial or social success? Are our actions themselves gratifying? By answering these questions in terms of our past choices, we can alleviate a lot of our dissatisfaction. Previous failures cannot deprive us—if we keep our values clear—of the open possibility of the present. Success is not something to strive for but something to enjoy. The danger is in closing off, at any point in our lives, the chance for another life-enriching choice.

Approval

From earliest childhood, we are taught to seek the approval of others. As we approach professional and personal maturity, the number of groups from which we seek approval and support presents a major dilemma. In two-career families one member's profession may have different values from the other. That divergence can be helpful to us. Once we realize that society is not a monolithic unit with unswerving regulations, we are free to determine for ourselves what will give us—individually and as a family unit—the deepest and most lasting satisfaction.

The ultimate approval is self-approval. Since we cannot always interpret the attitudes of those around us, we will find the only lasting approval in our family and among close friends. This approval is not so much for things that we do as for our integrity in maintaining our fundamental values.

Success

We asked Jill and Clayton why they stayed married if they were so dissatisfied with each other. "Because we want everyone to think we have a successful marriage," they said. This couple combined two basic values, neither of which made them happy. They sought approval from everyone because they thought that the appearance of success was more important than happiness, and they assumed that success depended on what other people thought of them.

Sometimes we may fool ourselves into believing that we are successful by imitating the visible signs of marital or professional success. We can keep up such a good front that no one knows the deep loneliness that exists in our marriage; and it is easy enough to talk big so that no one sees how little we have actually accomplished in our profession.

Beyond this synthetic success lies the true success that comes from a clear definition of purpose and the effort to accomplish that purpose. Jill and Clayton succeeded in giving others the impression they wanted. In practically every individual activity they had undertaken they had been successful. Yet their lives were unsatisfying because their own value system had not reached beyond the success stage.

Self-Fulfillment

Financial or even marital success does not automatically guarantee satisfaction. Real satisfaction is obtained as a by-product of our efforts. If we are involved in an interesting job or truly concerned about the welfare of someone else, we will become absorbed in our efforts. When someone asks us, "Are you successful?" we'll look surprised and say, "That's a silly question."

Success assumes a conclusion, but our most useful activity is never concluded. It is a continuous process that creates an illusion of eternity in the moment. Self-fulfillment is complete at each step along an endless path.

Sandra and Perry were a self-fulfilled couple. Here's how they went about it. When Perry was thirty-five, he had a heart attack. He and Sandra were working hard to pay for a $135,000 condominium. Their life was that of the successful young business couple. Sandra had built a chain of candy stores from a single hole-in-the-wall and was now wholesaler to a five-state area. Perry was regional representative for an electronics firm and taught management courses at night.

The heart attack changed everything. The doctor told Perry that he could not continue to put the kind of pressure on himself that he had been exerting. When he came home from the hospital, he and Sandra talked about their future. "We've been so busy working that we've never stopped to ask what we're working for," Sandra said. "Why have we been working so hard?"

Perry laughed weakly. "I've been so busy trying that I never had time to ask why. It seemed the thing to do." They agreed that the reason they worked was so they could enjoy life, and it was obvious that life wouldn't last long the way they were going.

When Perry recovered, he went back to work part time and gave up his teaching job. Sandra hired a manager and an accountant and spent half her time home with Perry. To their great surprise, they continued to do well, but with far less strain than before. They had not really changed their job descriptions appreciably, only their value system. Their health and their own relationship replaced success as their main objective.

Our dissatisfaction with life frequently arises because we are unsure why we are doing what we are doing. When we begin to see the reasons, we can work out our priority system and—if necessary—rearrange the value system from which our priorities are derived. Like Sandra and Perry, we may end up doing the same things we have been doing, but with more pleasure and profit.

ESTABLISHING PRIORITIES

When we know the reasons for our past choices, it's easier to make the next ones. Even if we make some of our choices because we want the prestige that goes with them, we are happier if we know that is our reason. Self-deception is a serious impediment to self-fulfillment.

Each day we are going to have to decide whether we want more money or more leisure, more time with the children or more time at the office, more prestige or more anonymity. These priorities are not something that we establish once and then forget. Every time we answer the phone or talk to someone, we are likely to be faced with a choice that demands a priority rating. By saying that we will take on another committee we clearly choose against some other possible use of our time.

Still, each choice we make fixes our priorities more firmly, because we get in the habit of favoring one area or another. Erica, for example, avoided her children because they made her nervous. She was not sure what to do with them. By making a series of commitments to social action groups and her job, she safely avoided responsibility for her two girls, whose upbringing then devolved upon their father, who was usually home in the evenings.

When the children were fourteen and sixteen, Erica tried to have a long talk with them. "Why have you always favored your father over me?" she asked them.

"You were always too busy for us," one of them said. "He had time to talk to us and you didn't."

Erica was surprised that her life had drawn her away from her girls, but her priority system had led her to avoid the responsibilities that made her feel insecure.

We don't always profit from doing just what we want to do. Sometimes our priorities are determined by a sense of duty that leads to a deeper satisfaction than flitting from one easy choice to the next. Unless we make a conscious effort to examine our priority system occasionally and make needed adjustments to it, we can end up like Erica—out of control.

BEING SATISFIED

If we know why we make our choices and continue to control our priorities, we are going to be satisfied. Being satisfied is quite different from being smug. Smug people are generally quite dissatisfied without knowing it. Their smugness is a defense against their basic fear that they are missing something. Satisfied people are happy anyway. They know that things will go wrong. They will be tired sometimes, irritated, thwarted, but their basic satisfaction with life remains. The satisfied person's central self stands upright, convinced that life is good.

At every stage of a two-career marriage—from the early years when the hours are long and the pay short to the later years when the energy is short and the investments complex—the partners counterbalance each other. When one is up psychologically, the other may be down; but the marital teeter-totter continues to shift position.

Satisfaction is not something we have only when things go right. It's what keeps us going when things go wrong. Lynn had always planned to be a journalist, but her marriage to Kip limited her choice of jobs. "I don't mind," she said. "I chose to marry, and I'm not sorry. There are other careers around here that will do equally well."

Soon she was working as a free-lance publicity manager for area political campaigns. In five years she had three people working for her in the state capital while she stayed home and did the organizing and fund raising.

At thirty-three she was so busy that she and Kip were rarely together in the evenings. "Don't you wish you could spend more time with each other?" we asked them one night at a party.

"I've chosen to take on this much work," Lynn said. "If I didn't enjoy the work, I'd find something else to do—like sit at home in the evenings with Kip. As it is, we are each doing what we most want to do. We're satisfied."

"Yes," Kip added. "If there's one thing I've learned from being married to Lynn, it's the danger of anticipatory living."

"What's anticipatory living?" we asked.

Lynn laughed. "It's what Kip calls the common failing in many marriages. When we were first married, Kip said, 'When we're really well-off, we'll go on a long vacation together.' That's when I told him about my theory of anticipatory living. You don't improve your life by waiting for something wonderful to happen. The something wonderful has to be happening right now or not at all. If you fill your present with anticipation, you are using up precious energy that should be spent on present joy."

Lynn's experience of planning for a career in journalism and shifting to a quite different one taught her not to live in the future. Living in anticipation of future pleasure only makes us dissatisfied with the present. As long as we are aware that we are making free choices—with some planning for the future with an emphasis on the present—we cultivate a creative satisfaction that generates energy rather than using it up.

HEALTH AND FATIGUE

Even the most satisfied people go through stages when poor health and fatigue dim their enthusiasm—especially in two-career families, where both are constantly trying to balance the public and the private spheres. In such families each partner may blame the other for problems that could be resolved with rest and a change of living habits.

Physical Pain

Dissatisfaction with life is often the result of physical pain. Something as simple as tooth decay has been known to destroy the marriage as well as the tooth. Backache, sinus headaches, and digestive problems are chronic conditions among managerial couples. They are often caused by—and contribute to—the tension in our lives. The unhappiness they build is difficult to overcome in the family and at work.

Most of these conditions are programmed into our lifestyle. We sit on uncomfortable chairs in stuffy offices and restaurants drinking coffee and smoking. Little wonder we end up with bad backs, bad stomachs, and bad heads. Although these conditions cannot be drastically changed, our attitude toward them can. We can begin by determining the amount of control we have over them. Many people who give up smoking find that they have fewer bad headaches. Those who give up coffee find their digestive problems diminish significantly.

Backache is more difficult to deal with. In the early stages, after the first two or three muscle spasms, a good exercise program can usually ease the pain. In later stages the back may require medical attention. A lot of people give lip service to exercise, but the fakes can usually be distinguished by their pasty faces and sagging paunches. When one of these people says, "I tried exercising for a year and it didn't help my back condition at all," ask him, "Did you exercise regularly?" The answer is invariably an embarrassed "Well, off and on."

You can't change your total life pattern, but you can take firm action against the physical ailments that afflict managerial couples. Fifteen minutes a day for exercise is better than fifteen days in hospital in traction. You may not think you can live without coffee, but ulcers and digestive problems can swing you toward Postum.

The choice is between an active, purposeful, controlled life or life as the victim of circumstance. Seeing the two possibilities should turn you toward bettering your health. Good health releases tension and improves your marriage.

Fatigue

Physical pain can make anyone wretched and dissatisfied. So can chronic fatigue. When Helen and Murray married, Helen thought

Murray had one of the sunniest dispositions she had ever known. He was always ready for a good time and a laugh. After they married, he became a section manager in a government agency where the competition for advancement to the supergrades was severe. Murray had prided himself on how little sleep he needed. After he helped Helen put the children to bed, he would sit down at his desk and plan for the next day. Then, even after he was in bed, he would lay awake for several hours mulling over personnel relationships that bothered him.

Murray remained a good father and husband, but after several years his disposition changed markedly. He was petulant and sulky, often making unreasonable demands on Helen and the children. They avoided him, so that instead of playing with the family after supper he immediately opened a beer and watched television. The children grew up around him, walking quietly when they were in his vicinity.

His moodiness carried over to his work. He lost his reputation as a fair manager and became noted for his irrational judgments and vindictiveness when someone wronged him. Helen was unable to involve him in social life. He became more and more the recluse. As his work declined in quality, he stopped staying up late to work on his plans for the next day; instead he stayed up late watching television. One night, when Helen came out to see why he didn't go to bed, she found him staring at a blank screen. She became worried and tried to get him to seek help from a counselor.

"I don't need a counselor," he muttered to her. "Why can't you let me alone?"

When his boss also suggested that he was not functioning well, he made an appointment. The psychiatrist told him that 8 percent of American men and 16 percent of American women suffer from debilitating depression of the sort he had. "It's an increased resentment at something you have lost," the psychiatrist told him. "In your case what you're losing is your youth, and you're scared about it. In your effort to retain your original energy, you burned yourself out. Over the years you have destroyed your healthy rest habits, and you have lost your good disposition at the same time."

With medication and some therapy, Murray reestablished good rest habits. When he did, his moodiness and depression disappeared. Helen, who had lost a lot of sleep over Murray, also began to sleep well again, and their middle years were happy ones.

Any number of conditions can cause loss of sleep, but when it starts happening regularly, you should do something about it. If you are unduly tired and still can't sleep, you should have a physical checkup. If you don't want to go to sleep, examine your life to find out where the trouble lies. You can gain control again. The choice is yours.

FAMILY COMPETITION

Internal competition is a major threat to satisfaction in two-career marriages. Such rivalry, when it is lighthearted and done in a spirit of love, may be all right. But frequently it can become a dangerous undercurrent that sweeps you into the waters of discontent. It is much wiser to turn your competitive efforts toward people at work and avoid competition at home, except in safe, limited areas.

Determining the safe areas is not always easy. Some couples can enter into violent competition at tennis or bridge and come away loving each other more than ever. Others carry the bad-loser syndrome into all their activities so that a family win means a family feud for the next week. More than one divorce has cited card table quarrels as its cause. If your competitive natures cause discontent, you should look deeper to see why you are competitive within the family. Most of the time the competition reflects a basic insecurity that makes petty triumphs essential for your continued psychic balance.

Unfortunately, these petty triumphs are self-defeating. The more you have, the more you want. You are jealous of anyone's win but your own. You gradually become so greedy for victory that you are browbeating your children into playing checkers and chortling wildly when you jump one of their men. If you have an unhealthy competitiveness at home, you have to locate the source of your insecurity. It may be in the social, the financial, or the emotional areas of your life. Look at each one and see whether that is the place you need to develop strength.

Social Insecurity

Social insecurity is widespread in managerial circles. When you are insecure in social situations, either in your professional or your private life, you tend to be overbearing and competitive. You become a specialist in the verbal put-down and enjoy making others feel small and in the wrong. Your snobbish attitude is only a cover for your insecurity about your social position.

Wives and husbands, fearful of trying their snobbery on anyone else, often cut each other up in social gatherings. The verbal slashing and scathing sarcasm are symptoms of a deep discontent. Such couples have to admit who they are, where they came from, and what their social aspirations are. When they have come to grips with these problems, they won't have to resort to self-destructive behavior.

Once these couples have defined their social needs, they can gravitate toward the kind of people who support rather than threaten them. They can then develop a group of close friends with whom they can express themselves without feeling competitive or defensive.

Financial Insecurity

Financial insecurity manifests itself differently from social insecurity. When you are insecure socially, you can still relate to your partner well at home. Only under the pressure of social situations are you likely to compete with your partner for the limelight or the killing phrase. Financial insecurity is constantly active. If you are jealous of your partner's every purchase, even buying the groceries becomes a source of emotional tension.

Financial insecurity endangers family welfare and results in psychological harm and sometimes physical violence. Frustrated husbands and wives fight with each other or beat their children in a desperate effort to tear their way out of their financial bind. When any sort of violence arises in the family, the first place to look is at the financial situation. Frequently the real cause of the disruption is a desire for more money.

Sometimes financial troubles can be overcome by establishing a realistic family budget that everyone accepts. If everyone participates in making the budget decisions, after a few months family squabbles will disappear. When the family crunch is relieved, security replaces insecurity.

Emotional Insecurity

Uncertainty about emotional ties is the most diffuse and difficult kind of insecurity. Knowing you are loved is more important than having social position or money. The other two take care of themselves when you are secure emotionally. But when you are insecure in your love relationships, you can never be satisfied, no matter how much social and financial success comes to you. Emotional insecurity expresses itself in many ways—in moodiness, physical complaints, fatigue.

Almost everything we've talked about so far in this chapter can be an indication of the need for more love.

The search for more love threatens the solidarity of the marriage. If the two of you do not find ways to express your affection, you will go elsewhere to be reassured that you are loved. You may retain an unhealthy tie with one or both of your parents to compensate for the lack of closeness in your marriage. You may compete for your children's love and pit them against one another. Or you and your partner may set up a competition match by taking lovers to show each other how much you are *really* loved.

All these competitions, obviously, result in increased dissatisfaction. They are unsatisfactory ways to resolve a sense of emptiness. It is essential to feel secure in your love. Love is the source of strength in your marriage. Your career, your finances, your children—all the aspects of your life that have meaning—have meaning only in terms of the love that you and your partner express to each other. Without that love, the rest of your efforts count for nothing.

How you communicate your love depends on how your parents demonstrated their love in your presence. If you had good models, you are lucky. Perpetuate them in your own love relationship. If your parents did not show you a good example, you will have to build your own tradition to transmit to your children.

That new tradition arises from an acceptance of the central importance of demonstrated love in your life. Two-career families work best when both careerists are working to support their love. Love doesn't mean just playing together or having sex together. It means sharing a pattern of existence in which you spend time together looking out at the world from the psychic shelter of your mutual concern.

You are constantly building a bigger and better playground in which to exercise your permanent commitment to each other. Together you are finding ways of understanding each other better, of helping each other more. And when you have accepted that reality of a two-career marriage, you will be satisfied even if the rest of the world collapses around you. You don't have to be Romeo and Juliet to look out from the secure balcony of your affection and name the new day that shines for you outside. You can be two careerists united as one, the truly married, who have fused the public and the private spheres of their lives with the holding power of their love.

The Joneses Talk About Dissatisfaction

Ruth: It seems to me we've spent a lot more time in this chapter on dissatisfaction than on satisfaction.

Bill: I guess that's because dissatisfaction is the active evil. Unless we can clear that away, we'll never be able to achieve the satisfaction we're longing for. After all, isn't satisfaction just another name for happiness?

Ruth: Perhaps, but happiness can never be dependent on everything's being fine, because then we would always be worried that it wouldn't stay that way. We're sometimes happy "in spite of" as well as "because of." I don't think that people can be happy in a chronic state of dissatisfaction.

Bill: We're working on the assumption that dissatisfaction is an unnatural state that can be corrected. We both know, though, that there are certain basically melancholy people who thrive on discontent. One person we know says that life is only a series of debasements, and another says it's a continuous series of painful experiences. Aren't these people happiest being unhappy?

Ruth: Some people are happy only when they're recounting their miseries. Still, I think that people should do all they can to erase the dissatisfactions from their own lives. If there is an objective reality you can't change, you have to be satisfied that you've done all you can and settle for that. I'm talking here about two different kinds of dissatisfaction. The first kind is dissatisfaction with your role in life; the second kind is dissatisfaction with external events.

Bill: Are you suggesting that one of these types of dissatisfaction is less destructive to a two-career marriage than the other?

Ruth: Yes. Compare the difference between being dissatisfied because you never had a chance to go into business for yourself and failing in the business once you start it. The first could be a gnawing disappointment that lasted all your life. The second can be accepted and dealt with as a valuable experience in discovering personal limitations.

Bill: That's an important distinction. The point, then, is that we must ferret out gnawing disappointments of the first sort as something we can't change and work positively through disappointments of the second sort that sometimes strengthen us in the long run.

Ruth: While we're ferreting out our disappointments of the first sort, we might find that with more courage or a substitution of goals we could do something about these too.

Bill: We've spent most of this discussion on disappointments, just as we did in the chapter, but I'm not disappointed. I think you've made the central point this book is about. If we know what we want and how to get it, we'll know whether our goal is realistic or not. If it's not, we have to look for a more reasonable goal. When we find one, we go after it in a happy, satisfied way—together—as you and I have gone about finishing this book.

Index